The Spectacular Library of Magical Things

Also by Caroline Busher

The Ghosts of Magnificent Children

The Girl Who Ate the Stars

The Legend of Valentine Sorrow

Votes for Women! The Irish Women's Suffrage Movement

The Spectacular Library of Magical Things

Caroline Busher

POOLBEG

Published 2022
by Poolbeg Press Ltd
123 Grange Hill, Baldoyle
Dublin 13, Ireland
E-mail: poolbeg@poolbeg.com

Typesetting, editing, layout, design, ebook © Poolbeg Press Ltd.

1

A catalogue record for this book is available from the British Library.

ISBN 978-1-78199-707-9

Typeset by Poolbeg.

Printed by CPI Group, UK

www.poolbeg.com

About the Author

Caroline Busher graduated with a First Class Honours MA in Creative Writing from UCD. She adores reading and writing fantastical stories. Caroline lives in Ireland with her husband John and her children Fiachra, Keeva and Tiernan. She writes her books in an eighteenth-century-style shepherd's hut, nestled beneath the Blackstairs Mountains. Caroline believes that it is the most magical place on earth. But be warned: The mountains resemble sleeping giants and legend has it that they might wake up someday.

Caroline is an Irish Times Bestselling Author. Her books include *The Ghosts of Magnificent Children*, *The Girl Who Ate the Stars*, *The Legend of Valentine Sorrow* (which was shortlisted for the Teen Book of the Year at the An Post Irish Book Awards in 2021) and *Votes for Women! The Irish Women's Suffrage Movement* (all published by Poolbeg Press). She is represented by Trace Literary Agency (USA).

Acknowledgements

When I was a little girl, my father told me the story of the Banshee. The most profound female figure in Irish folklore. He said that I if I found a comb on the road I should never pick it up as it could belong to the Banshee. I have spoken to people who claim to have heard the cry of the Banshee. I have heard descriptions of a wailing woman with long white hair. However, I have always wondered what life would be like for a young banshee. I wanted to tell the story about the girl behind the legend and her struggle to survive in a world where she is misunderstood.

Then, when I was writing *The Spectacular Library of Magical Things* something incredible happened. I encountered an old Irish Tradition that really sparked my imagination. Long ago in Ireland, during the summer months groups of teenage girls would go up into the mountains. They would live together in stone huts called Booley Houses. Many stayed there until Halloween. However, there are some accounts of unexplained occurrences up on those windswept mountains. Some of those stories involved the Banshee. I decided to set my novel in County Wexford against the backdrop of the battle of Vinegar Hill in 1798. Expect mythical islands, a girl with a wing, a spectacular library and most importantly await the story of a young banshee who discovers that there is power in her cry and once it is released it cannot be contained.

I am so incredibly grateful to everyone in Poolbeg Press, especially to Paula Campbell who has always believed in me and my writing. She has encouraged me to be the best writer I can be. Thank you so much, Paula. You work so hard, and I am very grateful for everything that you have done for me. Sincere thanks to my incredible editor Gaye Shortland who cares as much about my books as I do. You are wonderful, Gaye. Thank you so much for your care and attention to detail which has made my books more spectacular than I ever dreamed possible. To my wonderful literary agent Tracy Brennan. Thank you for being with me every step of the way, Tracy, and for getting my books into the right hands. You are a pleasure to work with.

Sincere thanks to Wexford County Council Arts Department and to Artlinks for awarding me Literature Bursaries. Your continued support of my practice has enabled me to develop my craft as a writer.

Deepest thanks to Wexford Public Library Services – to Eileen Morrissey and Hazel Percival and to all the librarians and staff who have supported me on my journey as a writer. Libraries are the beating heart of the community – to all the library services across Ireland, you are amazing. Thank you for everything you do to encourage reading and for getting books into the hands of young people.

Huge thanks to Wexford Literary Festival for always supporting my practice as a writer and for promoting writing in County Wexford.

We are incredibly blessed in Ireland to have so many fantastic booksellers. Thank you all so much for everything that you do to promote books. A very special thanks to Amy Devereux in Wexford Book Centre who is one of the kindest and most knowledgeable book people I know!

To the writing community in Ireland, thank you. I have met so many amazing writers over the last few years. Your support and encouragement have been invaluable. A very special thanks to Elizabeth Murray, who is one of my greatest friends and writes amazing books!

Thank you so much to Alan McGuire on South East Radio. Alan, you are so supportive of my writing, and I really appreciate it.

To each and every schoolteacher in Ireland. You are truly inspirational and work so hard every day to encourage young people to read. Thank you for reading my books to your students.

And to my family:

Thank you to my beautiful parents Séamus and Kathleen Doyle. I love you both more than you could ever know. I am incredibly blessed to be your daughter. I could not ask for better parents. Thank you for all the stories that you told to me growing up, for taking me to the library and for buying books which sparked my imagination.

To my husband John. You are my best friend and such a talented artist. Thank you so much for believing in me and for supporting me in everything I do. I am lucky to have you in my life.

To my three incredible children:

Fiachra: I am so proud of you and the wonderful young man that you have become. You are so intelligent and kind and inspire me every day. May all your dreams come true. You deserve the very best that life has to offer.

Keeva: Having you as my daughter is a blessing. You are so creative, kind and talented and teach me so much about caring for the planet that we live on. I love visiting vintage-clothes stores with you and having coffee and cake in our favourite café. I love you with all my heart, my wonderful girl.

Tiernan: Thank you for being such an amazing son. You inspire me every day. You are so creative, clever, fun and energetic and have the kindest heart. I am so lucky to be your mother.

To all my family in Ireland and England. To all my aunts, uncles, cousins and in-laws, thank you for always being there for me. Thank you so much to my father-in-law John for always being so supportive and encouraging.

Thank you to all my friends and neighbours. I am very lucky to have so many wonderful people in my life.

As always, extra-special thanks to my three best friends, Clare Fletcher, Helena Dunbar and Patricia McNally. Your friendship means the world to me.

Last but not least, a huge thank-you to readers for picking up my book and reading it. A book only comes to life when it is read. I hope that you have as much enjoyment reading *The Spectacular Library of Magical Things* as I did writing it!

Dedication

I would like to dedicate this book to my family.
To my parents Séamus and Kathleen, my husband
John and my children Fiachra, Keeva and Tiernan.

Part One

THE SONG OF THE BOOLEY GIRLS

We are seven

seven are we

friends forever

forever we will be

alone on the mountains

singing our song,

green mist descended

everything went wrong,

so come up and find us

if you dare,

the Booley Girls of Wexford

will meet you there.

Chapter one

THE GIRL WITH A WING

It was a star-filled night when Banshee Island erupted through the mist. Golden comets streamed across the sky like acrobats. Cara longed to travel to the island.

She stood on the shore. Her pale-blue nightdress and dressing-gown billowed in the breeze. Her silky black hair danced over her shoulders. Waves lapped against her ankles. Cara was no ordinary girl. She was born with a wing instead of an arm. Long white feathers stretched from one of her shoulder blades. They were as smooth as the translucent sea glass that washed up on the shore.

Cara had heard stories about the magic on Banshee Island and she was drawn to it like the wind to a fire.

According to legend, Banshee Island appeared once every seven years just before the summer solstice. Folklore said that the mysterious island was home to a banshee, a spirit who took the souls of the dead to the afterlife.

Cara stretched her extensive wing and allowed the sea breeze to dance between her feathers. They fluttered as she moved. She could not help but wonder if the magical island would be more suited to a girl like her. A girl who was as much a bird as a human. A girl who did not fit in on the Land of the Living.

"Who do we have here?"

Cara screamed. She covered her wing with her dressing gown. It was a reflex, an act of self-preservation, something she always did when others were near. Cara turned to face Mr Crooks. His large, angry eyes bulged like planets in their sockets. Veins lined his eyeballs. He had a face like thunder and a long grey beard, adorned with bits of food that had fallen from his mouth. He carried his rifle and his pet raven Storm was perched on his left shoulder. The bird was every bit as cantankerous as the old man.

Cara guessed that the bird was jealous of her wing when she looked at his own dishevelled plumage. At least you can fly, she thought.

"I–I was just looking at the island, Mr Crooks," Cara stammered.

Then she blinked away the tears from her fierce blue eyes, which were tucked like secrets beneath long dark eyelashes. Cara didn't like Mr Crooks one bit. He had worked for her family for as long as she could remember. He lived in a small wooden hut on the edge of the estate and he worked for her family as a gardener and a gamekeeper. Sometimes Cara heard the ping of the bullets from his rifle as he shot unsuspecting birds from the sky. It made her feathers bristle just thinking of it.

"No good will come of looking at Banshee Island. The banshee will come for you. Just like she came for the Booley Girls. Mark my words. She is drawn to freaks like you!" Mr Crooks pointed his bony finger at Cara.

The bird flapped his scruffy wings in agreement.

Traitor, Cara thought, as she stared into the bird's glassy eyes.

"I have to go now, Mr Crooks. Goodbye!"

Cara's heart thumped loudly in her chest as she ran back through the gates to Soul Shadow Manor. She darted from side to side in case Crooks decided to turn his rifle on her.

Statues of stone angels lined the winding driveway. The crumbling manor house had been in Cara's father's family for generations. Cara ran up the stone steps two at a time and her wing trailed on the floor as she swept into the large entrance hall. She narrowly avoided bumping into Spellfinder, the cranky housekeeper, who was carrying a silver tray of drinks into the ballroom.

Spellfinder detested Cara. Nothing Cara did was ever good enough. Cara knew that it was because of her wing. When Cara was younger, Spellfinder used to pluck out her feathers and use them to stuff pillowcases. *"There must be an arm under there somewhere!"* she would hiss. However, Cara's feathers always grew back and eventually Spellfinder stopped plucking them.

Spellfinder's face was covered in small, round bumps. Her nose was crooked and her front tooth was chipped. She wore her black hair short and around her neck hung a small silver pendant shaped like a hare.

There was something about Spellfinder that scared Cara. Sometimes when she went to the beach, she saw Spellfinder and Mr Crooks huddled together like a pair of dishevelled crows. It would not surprise her one bit if the wicked pair were plotting a way to get rid of her once and for all.

"Cara, did you hear what I said?"

"I'm sorry, Mrs Spellfinder?"

"Get to bed right away, young miss. Your father is

entertaining very important guests. He doesn't need any of your nonsense tonight."

Mrs Spellfinder put the tray down on a table and opened the door to the ballroom. The sound of music and laughter escaped. Cara caught sight of a woman in a beautiful green ballgown with a large pink bow tied around the waist. Her long slender arms were outstretched as a man twirled her around the dancefloor. She reminded Cara of a ballerina in a music box.

Tears sprang to Cara's eyes. She realised that she would never be asked to dance. Who would want to dance with a girl with a wing? *"Freaks like you!"* Mr Crook's words spun like silk in her mind. She sighed loudly then she pushed the worrying thoughts from her head, in the way that mountains push away rainclouds that settle on their shoulders moments before a storm.

She ran as fast as she could up the marble staircase. Paintings of her ancestors, the lords and ladies of Soul Shadow Manor, loomed down from a great height. Not one of them had a wing like her. All of the girls had dainty hands and long slim arms. She had inherited her wing from her mother's side of the family, a colony of shapeshifting swans. Cara had never met them. Her mother abandoned her when she was a baby. The colony of swans did not want anything to do with her.

7

They were ashamed of her. Her father said that they would peck her eyes out if she met them.

Cara's bedroom overlooked the sea. It had the best view in the house. Two glass doors opened up onto an enormous balcony. She picked up her silver binoculars from her swan-shaped dressing table and stepped outside. The moon peered down like a torch, illuminating Banshee Island. Cara gazed through her binoculars. In the distance, she could see the silhouette of golden swans flying through the air. Legend said that the swans were called 'Soul Dancers' as they carried the souls of the dead to the afterlife. They were a magnificent sight.

If only I was born a swan instead of the freak that I am, Cara thought. Then I could fly to Banshee Island.

Suddenly, to her surprise, she noticed someone on the island. It was a girl. A real girl. Her hair was as white as snow. The girl was standing on the shore. She wore red trousers and large black boots. She was pointing a spyglass in her direction.

She couldn't be the banshee – she was too young. Could the banshee have a daughter?

"Who are you?" Cara cried. Her words danced like starlings in the wind.

Suddenly Cara's bedroom door burst open. Kitty the chambermaid bounded in. She wore a long black dress and a white frilly apron. She wore her mousy-brown hair tied up in a ponytail that swished from side to side when she walked. Cara liked Kitty. She was from County Kilkenny and she had moved to Wexford to live with her aunt. Cara's father found it hard to get local people to work for them, due to Cara's strange affliction. They were also rumoured to be haunted by a ghost. It was one of the reasons that Cara struggled to make any friends. When she was younger she said that she could see the ghost – a young girl dressed in a long red skirt, with a blue shawl around her shoulders. Her father said that it was nothing more than an imaginary friend. However, occasionally a young girl floating up the stairs, or standing at the window in the nursery, was seen by the servants.

Kitty placed a hand on Cara's shoulder. "Spellfinder sent me to check on you, Cara. You must go to bed. We're going to Enniscorthy tomorrow."

"Enniscorthy? Do we have to? I prefer it here by the sea. And Father said that the sea air is good for Grammy's health."

"Enniscorthy is your home, Cara. We had lots of fun there last summer. Don't you remember sailing on the River Slaney? Or the time we climbed up Vinegar Hill?"

Cara's heart sank like a rock in the ocean as she shut

the balcony door with a bang. She placed her hand on her wing. The feathers felt soft beneath her finger and thumb. She walked over to her dressing-table and sat down on the small pink-velvet stool. Soul Shadow Manor was the family's summer residence. Cara hated the thought of going back to the cold castle in Enniscorthy. Besides, her father had told her that there would be a great battle soon and that they all had to be prepared. "Every man, woman and child will have to play their part, Cara," he had said.

Everyone except me, Cara thought. What use would a girl with a wing be to anyone? The only thing she was good for was being laughed at and plucked for pillows.

Cara didn't understand why people needed to fight. Her father said that it was to stop the men in red coats from ruling Ireland. Her father was one of the leaders and he had an important job to do, which meant that Cara would have to help out too. Cara sighed. Then she turned to face Kitty who was humming a haunting tune.

Kitty picked up a silver hairbrush from the dressing-table. Then she carefully brushed out the knots from Cara's long black hair. When she had finished she picked up a silk cloth and ran it along Cara's feathers until they shone under the candlelight.

Cara caught Kitty's eye in the mirror.

"Tell me again everything you know about Banshee Island, Kitty."

Kitty smiled. She wanted to make Cara happy and would do anything to please her.

"All I know is that it mysteriously appears once every seven years, just before the summer solstice and it vanishes again on Midwinter's Eve."

"Father told me that no one has ever set foot on the island."

"Your father is right, Cara. No one living anyway. Many people have tried over the years, but as soon as they approach the shore the island vanishes before their eyes. And that's not all. They say that those people never have a day of luck in their lives afterwards."

"I would love to go to the island, Kitty, wouldn't you?"

"You are a strange girl, Cara. There is nothing for the living in that place. Why on earth would you want to go there?"

Cara wanted to ask Kitty about the girl she had seen on the island but some instinct stopped her.

"To meet the banshee and perhaps there are others there like me."

"What do you mean when you say others like you?"

"You know, children with wings. You must have seen

11

the swans flying through the sky, Kitty. Sometimes I feel as though I belong with them."

"Nonsense, Cara. You wouldn't last five minutes with swans for company. Having a wing doesn't make you a swan. They are not as much fun as me."

Cara smiled.

"And as for the banshee, well, she only comes to people who are going to die, Cara. Not healthy young girls like you."

"What about the Booley Girls? Didn't the banshee come for them?"

Kitty gasped. "You must not talk of the Booley Girls, Cara! It will bring bad luck."

"The children in school say that my Aunt Róisín was a Booley Girl. They say that means I am cursed. That is why they won't play with me – that, and my wing."

"Those children spend too much time listening to the superstitions of their parents." Kitty sighed. She felt sorry for Cara. It was true that her aunt was one of the Booley Girls. It was no wonder she had no friends.

"Tell me the truth about them, Kitty. I am begging you."

"The truth about who?"

"The Booley Girls."

"Alright. I will tell you everything that I know. But you must promise that you will never mention them again. And you must never tell anyone that I told you this or I could lose my job."

Cara's eyes opened wide and she quickly crossed her heart. "Cross my heart, I will never tell anyone, Kitty."

"Very well. It was Midsummer's Eve thirty years ago. There was a full moon in the sky. It was customary for young girls to go up into the mountains, to live together for the summer months. Girls all over Ireland had done this for years."

"It sounds very exciting. Why did they go into the mountains?"

"They took cows with them, to feed on the long green grass high up on the mountainside. They would spend their days milking the cows, singing songs and knitting. They lived in small stone houses."

"Were they not frightened up on the mountains all alone? Anything could happen to them."

"Yes, anything could. The girls often reported seeing strange supernatural occurrences on those mountainsides."

"Like what?"

"Sometimes they saw hares shapeshifting into witches

and wolves would prowl around at night. However, the girls were always safe until that dreadful Midsummer Night thirty years ago. Seven girls from Enniscorthy went up to Mount Leinster. None of them returned."

"Perhaps a wolf ate them?"

"No, Cara. A wolf would have left something behind. It was as if the girls were never there at all."

"My Aunt Róisín *was* one of the Booley Girls, wasn't she?"

"Yes, Cara, she was. They say your Aunt Róisín was the most special of them all, as she was the seventh daughter of a seventh daughter. This meant that she had a special gift. She could heal people of any illness."

"I didn't know that about Aunt Róisín. No one ever mentioned it to me before."

"Well, I shouldn't be telling you but I think you deserve to know."

"Do you think that I could heal people too?"

"Perhaps, Cara. However, whatever you were put on this earth to do will all be revealed in time."

"Why doesn't Father tell me about any of this? I knew Róisín went missing but I never knew how or where."

"Because he misses Róisín. You know she was his twin sister. It makes him sad to think of her."

"And that's why Grammy is so unhappy all the time?"

Kitty sighed. Mrs O'Leary never got over losing her only daughter. The old lady was bedridden. She blamed herself for letting Róisín go with the Booley Girls. However, people were always visiting her daughter, asking her to heal them when they were sick. People travelled from all over Ireland to visit the girl with the gift. Mrs O'Leary thought that sending her daughter to the mountains for the summer would give Róisín a break from all that. Never in her wildest dreams did she imagine that she would never see her daughter again.

"Yes. That is why even to this day she wears a black veil. She is still mourning her loss."

"What happened to the Booley Girls?"

"No one knows. They just disappeared. Many people have searched the mountains over the years in the hope that they would find them – however, they have found nothing. Not a trace of them. Many people blame the banshees, of course."

Suddenly there was a loud bang against the window.

"What on earth was that?" Kitty screamed. Then she clasped her hands to her heart.

"It was a bird, Kitty." Birds often slapped against

Cara's window. Many of them died. Others she was able to save. Birds were drawn to her.

"Don't you think it's odd the way birds do that to you, Cara?"

"What?"

"Throw themselves against your window."

"I thought the birds did that to everyone, Kitty."

"No, Cara. They don't."

Cara shrugged. "Perhaps it is because I am a bird like them."

"How many times do I have to tell you, Cara? Having a wing does not make you a bird!"

"Do you blame the banshee on the island, Kitty? For what happened to the Booley Girls?"

"It's hard to know, Cara. I wouldn't like to point the finger at anyone."

"I wonder where the Booley Girls went to?"

"Who knows? Farmers have said that sometimes late at night they hear the sounds of girls singing sweetly on the mountainside. However, when they follow the sound they discover that there is no one there."

"How peculiar!"

"Yes, it is," Kitty agreed as turned down the blankets on Cara's four-poster bed.

"What do the Booley Girls sing, Kitty?"

"They sing their curse. It goes like this …

We are seven
seven are we
friends forever
forever we will be
alone on the mountains
singing our song,
green mist descended
everything went wrong,
so come up and find us
if you dare,
The Booley Girls of Wexford
will meet you there."

"Oh, that's so haunting, and you sing it so beautifully!"

"Thank you – but I have told you enough for one night, Cara. Stretch your wing and then get to bed."

"Do you think the banshee ever gets lonely, Kitty?"

"I don't know. I have never thought about it before."

"Maybe she's not alone? Maybe she has a daughter or sister there?" She still didn't want to ask directly about the girl she had seen.

"Not that I've ever heard of. Now, get into bed, Cara!"

Cara yawned, stretched her wing, and hopped into bed.

17

Kitty tucked her in and then she walked over to the window.

"Can you leave my curtains open tonight, please, Kitty? I want to look at the moon."

"Alright then. As long as you go to sleep and no more talk about the Booley Girls or the banshee, do you hear me?"

Kitty smiled at Cara. She could not help but feel sorry for her. In all the years that she had worked for the family she had never seen Cara with any friends and Cara's grandmother, Rose, was so sad all of the time. People said that Cara looked just like her Aunt Róisín and seeing her granddaughter every day made Rose O'Leary sad. Cara reminded her of the daughter she had lost, all those years ago.

When Kitty applied for the position of chambermaid people warned her against it.

"I wouldn't work for that family for all the gold in the world," they said. "The ghost of a Booley Girl haunts them. She wanders around the rooms during the night, begging for someone to save her."

"And what kind of a girl is born with a wing? It's not natural. The Good Lord would never make such a strange creature."

Kitty believed in ghosts but she wasn't scared of them.

So she took the position at Soul Shadow Manor, much to the dismay of her friends and family. Sometimes late at night, Kitty heard peculiar sounds coming from the attic and wondered if it could be the ghost.

She placed her hand on Cara's head. It was no wonder that she was such a strange child, with all this talk of ghosts and a wing for an arm. Her father's role as one of the leaders of the Wexford United Irishmen meant that he was away most of the time and that big old castle that they owned in Enniscorthy was cold and no place for a child.

"Sweet dreams, little one," Kitty whispered.

Then as she turned to walk out of the room, she thought she saw a young girl sitting at the dressing-table. Kitty placed her hand over her mouth and ran out of the room as fast as she could. Although she wasn't scared of the ghost of Soul Shadow Manor, she didn't want to disturb her.

Cara was left with just the moon, a headful of dreams and the ghost of a Booley Girl for company.

Chapter two

BANSHEE ISLAND

An hour before

Síofra was a girl who guided the souls of the dead to the afterlife. She lived with her aunt on Banshee Island, a murky and tempestuous place in the middle of the foreboding sea.

Their house was built from the wood of pirate ships that were shipwrecked on the shore. It was painted red and jutted out of the cliff-face like a wart on a giant's chin. The house could only be reached by climbing up two hundred stone steps that were carved out centuries earlier by a warrior queen who rode a white horse. The house was guarded by the wooden figurehead of a fearless dragon which had washed up on the shore. It had previously clung to the helm of a Viking ship that sank like a sea creature beneath the merciless waves during a beast of a storm. The bones of the Vikings lay in a graveyard beneath the sea and their ghosts haunted the area.

Síofra's companions were the ghost of a fox cub with piercing green eyes, her Aunt Silver and the souls of the dead.

Síofra peered through the ancient silver spyglass that her aunt had given to her as an early birthday present and gasped. In the distance, with a mile of water between them, was a girl with jet-black hair and piercing blue eyes. Síofra noticed an extraordinary thing. The girl had a wing instead of an arm. She held out the wing and the long white feathers swayed in the breeze. The girl's lips moved and for a moment it felt as though time stood still. Síofra longed to walk across the water and talk to her.

"You must never make friends with the living, Síofra," Aunt Silver had cautioned her recently. "That is how your mother disappeared all those years ago when you were just a baby."

"What was my mother like, Aunt Silver?" Síofra had asked.

"Why must you keep on asking me the same questions over and over again, Síofra?"

"Because when you talk about my mother it makes me feel close to her. You are lucky, Silver. You remember her."

Silver sighed. Her heart went out to Síofra. She longed to know about her mother and who her father was. However, the truth of what happened all those years ago had broken Silver's heart. She kept silent in order to protect Síofra. But she realised that Síofra was getting older now and she would have to answer her questions sooner or later.

"Your mother was the most powerful banshee to have ever lived, Síofra, and she could stop the hands of time with her cry. Banshees came from islands all over Ireland, just to meet her. You are like her, Síofra, and you will be as powerful as she was one day, believe me."

Now Síofra peered through her silver spyglass at the girl one more time. "Who are you? she murmured and the breeze carried her voice from deep within her lungs, out of her throat and up into the star-filled sky.

The girl reached out her wing. Her hair billowed in the breeze. Suddenly the waves formed white peaks like tiny mountains. The wind howled and swallowed Síofra's thoughts of the girl whole.

Síofra placed her ancient spyglass into her pocket.

Then she steadied herself as she prepared to welcome a new soul to Banshee Island. The soul belonged to an old woman. Her eyes were deep-set. Her cheeks were lined like a map. But she was overjoyed. Her old bones didn't creak anymore. She hadn't walked without a stick for years. She felt young again and as light as a feather. Golden light streamed from her eyes. A huge smile beamed on her face as she drifted up into the air. Síofra reached out and gripped the old lady's ankle, gently pulling her back down to earth. It was not unusual for souls to drift away. They had not got used to being free of their bodies yet. However, it was not time for the woman to move on, or else she would not have arrived on Banshee Island. The woman needed memories from her earthly life to ground her and to stop her from floating away altogether. On the days leading up to a soul's arrival on Banshee Island, objects from their lives would wash up on the shore. Síofra gathered them and Silver stored them in The Spectacular Library of Magical Things. This ancient library was guarded by a flock of one-eyed magpies. Síofra was forbidden from entering it. Silver told her the magic it contained could be dangerous if it fell into the wrong hands.

This old lady owned an assortment of curiosities, and each one told a story about her life. There was a taxidermy crow with a worm in its beak, a wind-up musical box and the ear of a goat. Síofra enjoyed guessing the significance of each of the wonders. The objects a person owns in their lifetime contain part of the person's essence.

"Where am I?" the woman inquired.

"You are on Banshee Island."

"That means I am dead, doesn't it?"

Silver had told Síofra that she must always answer the soul's questions truthfully, even though the truth was often a bitter pill to swallow.

"Yes, you are dead. But please don't be frightened. Many have walked this road before you and many will come after."

The old woman looked Síofra up and down. What a strange-looking girl, she thought. Síofra wore a pair of red trousers with a matching waistcoat. On her feet were a pair of large black boots and her thick white hair was cut just above her shoulders. The old woman had almost mistaken her for a boy. However, her white hair spoke of another tale. A tale that she had heard many times. The tale of the Banshee.

"If this is Banshee Island then you must be a banshee?" she asked.

Síofra nodded. Although it was only partly true.

Síofra was not a fully-fledged banshee yet. Not until she found her cry. The wait was exasperating. Silver had found her cry on the eve of her thirteenth birthday. Síofra's thirteenth birthday was just three days from now. The thought of being a banshee with her own Island of Souls to care for scared and excited her in equal measure.

The old lady's heart sank like an anchor into the seabed. "I can't be dead. I didn't get a chance to say goodbye to everyone. My daughter and my grandchildren will miss me so much!"

The smile drifted from her mouth like a cloud across the sun. Silver had a feather. It came from the Library of Magical Things and belonged to an ancient race of shapeshifting swans who inhabited Banshee Island at the beginning of time. The ancient swans could shapeshift into humans. The swans living on Banshee Island now had lost that ability. The shapeshifting swans had the most beautiful song until one day when witches stole their song from them. Silver wished she knew where to find it. Silver wore the swan's feather in a purple top hat. She believed that the ancient feather brought her luck.

Every banshee had a special celebration called a crying ceremony. Síofra could not wait for hers.

During the crying ceremony banshees from all over Ireland would flock together to hear the new banshee's cry. Silver had prepared her well for life as a banshee. "Everyone living and dead has fears, Síofra. Kindness and patience are the only way to help them," Silver had explained.

Síofra gently held the old woman's hand and smiled at her. It always astounded her how the souls looked exactly the same as they did when they were alive.

"Can the living not see the souls of the dead, Aunt Silver?" Síofra had asked one windswept afternoon as a rainbow cascaded across the light-blue sky.

"Only a banshee can see what a person's soul looks like, Síofra. It shines like gold dust in their ribcage. We have a special gift. I know the exact moment when a person will leave their life behind. You will know it too one day."

Thunder rumbled in the sky. Síofra looked up and an egg-shaped moon shone down. A rustle in the trees told Síofra that they were not alone. The ghost of her fox cub, Niamh, bounded through the trees. The moonlight illuminated the golden hues in the animal's coat. It glistened in the moonlight. Niamh bounded into Síofra's open arms. "It is good to see you too,

Niamh," Síofra said as the little fox rubbed her wet nose against her neck.

She placed Niamh on the ground again.

"This way," she said gently to the old woman.

Then she guided the old woman's soul to the edge of a golden river where an ancient hawthorn tree erupted like starlight through the earth. The branches were adorned with vibrant ribbons. Green, blue, pink, purple, yellow, red and orange. Souls that arrived hung ribbons on the tree to remind them of precious moments from their lives.

Síofra reached into the old leather satchel that she wore slung across her shoulder. After a moment of rummaging she pulled out two red ribbons, and then she traced her finger across the withered palm of the old woman's hand.

"I have a gift for you. But first I must take your name."

"My name is Peggy O'Reilly."

"You are very welcome here, Peggy. In giving me your name you are taking the first step towards leaving the Land of the Living behind you."

Then she handed Peggy the first ribbon, which Peggy tied to a low branch on the old oak tree.

Peggy smiled. "Once when I was a little girl, my parents took me to the Zoological Gardens. It was

Easter time. Mother wore a lovely straw bonnet and Daddy wore his best suit."

Suddenly a vision of Peggy O'Reilly as a young girl materialised in the night sky. She had a head full of brown curls. She clung to her parents' hands. They swung her through the air.

Peggy was astounded. There in the night sky above her was an image of her parents. A tear fell from her eye.

Síofra handed Peggy another ribbon, which she tied to a branch further up the tree.

"I remember my wedding day to my beloved John, God rest his soul. Both our families were there and he looked so handsome in his suit. I felt like the luckiest woman on earth."

Síofra followed Peggy's gaze as she peered up towards the heavens. The vision of Peggy and John O'Reilly on their wedding day burst through the clouds. They were standing on the steps outside a church. Síofra could hear the church bell ring. They made a lovely couple.

Suddenly the vision disappeared.

Síofra looked at Peggy who seemed to be cheerful again.

She led her along a path in the forest, Niamh following at their heels.

They came to a signpost.

"Follow that sign, Peggy. It will take you to the waiting-room."

"A waiting-room?"

"Yes, Peggy. You will then fly on the back of a golden swan. It will take you onwards to your final destination."

"Heaven!" Peggy said. Tears streamed down her cheeks as she realised she would be reunited with her parents and her husband John once more.

"I hope that you find everything you wish for, Peggy," Síofra said. Although she could not be sure of what awaited Peggy, she hoped that it would be something good.

"*Go raibh maith agat*, child," Peggy said. "Thank you."

Síofra watched as Peggy drifted along the path as many had before her. Golden comets streamed across the sky. A golden swan plunged through the heart-shaped clouds and Síofra thought of the girl on the Land of the Living with the wing for an arm. If only she could reach her!

"*Goodbye, Peggy. Safe travels!*"

Níamh bounded off into the trees. Síofra knew that the small fox was no more than a ghost. One day she would leave too. That was the price you paid for loving someone on Banshee Island.

As soon as Peggy disappeared from sight, Síofra turned and ran towards the old graveyard where she knew Silver would be waiting for her.

Chapter three

LOST IN THE MISTS OF TIME

Síofra leapt over the ancient metal gate and then tiptoed past crumbling tombstones. The souls who lay beneath the tombs were long gone. All that was left was a pile of bones. In the midst of the tombstones was a beautiful stone angel, with wings outstretched. The angel was playing a harp and was standing beside a beautiful rosebush that bloomed all year round. Síofra loved to sit at the angel's feet and write poems.

Aunt Silver was standing next to the stone angel. The magical feather in her hat fluttered in the breeze. The golden beads strung on her elaborate skirt, which was made from peacock feathers, jangled in the wind. Sadbh, the soul of a brown owl, was perched on her left arm. In her right hand she held a small green bottle that allowed her to see into the invisible realm. Silver's long white hair matched Síofra's but hers flowed down to her ankles. She wore a cloak embroidered with images of an evergreen forest. There were shimmering lakes and ancient oak trees, birds singing in the sky and giant mountains. The cloak stretched out behind her and carpeted the ground.

Silver turned to face Síofra. Tears tumbled from her large green eyes.

Síofra plucked a rose from the bush beside the stone angel and offered it to her aunt who took the rose and held it close to her heart.

"What are you thinking about, Aunt Silver? You look so sad."

Silver sighed. "A long time ago, Síofra," she said, "a girl arrived on Banshee Island. She had flowing locks of black hair. The girl was so sad. She arrived here on the eve of her thirteenth birthday. She said that she had got lost on a mountain and could not find her way home."

"How dreadful!"

"Yes, Síofra, it was – and that is why I never told you when you were younger. But now, it's time I told you a number of things. You are at last ready to hear them." She sighed deeply again. "This girl ... during her time here we became great friends. We'd watch dolphins swimming during the daytime and in the evening we'd sit together by this stone angel and watch the sun set over the island."

"You must have been heartbroken when she left, Aunt Silver."

"I was, Síofra. However, she did not leave the island on the back of a golden swan. I think that she returned to the Land of the Living."

"Why would she do such a thing? Choosing to go back can be dangerous. She may never get the chance to return here again."

Silver sighed "I don't think that she chose to go back, Síofra. She simply disappeared in a green mist. The girl was lost in the Mists of Time. Her soul hadn't left her body. I had never met anyone like her before. I hope that she found her way home."

"What a tragic story!"

"Yes, it is. I think about her sometimes. Her name was Róisín. The day she left, this beautiful rosebush bloomed. It reminds me of her."

Síofra suddenly thought of the girl she had seen earlier.

"I saw a girl through my new spyglass, Aunt Silver. A girl on the Land of the Living. An extraordinary girl who had a wing instead of an arm! She was on a balcony of a big house and she had binoculars. She seemed to be looking directly at me and she said something. I think it means something. Perhaps she was calling me."

An alarmed look fell like a shadow across the banshee's face. She placed her hand gently on Síofra's cheek. "You are mistaken, Síofra. Only banshees are called to cry for the living before they die. You are not a banshee yet."

"What you are saying is true, Aunt Silver. I am not a fully grown banshee yet. However, the feelings I had when I saw the girl were very strong. I feel as though an invisible thread connects us."

Silver sighed. "It is only natural that you should feel this way, Síofra, but how many times have I told you that you must not make friends with the living? And you are not a banshee yet. Your time will come soon. Then you could go to her if she truly called you."

Síofra folded her arms across her chest and stamped her foot in frustration. Sadbh flapped her wings, twisted her neck and flew into the branches of a nearby hawthorn tree.

Síofra followed Silver out of the graveyard. They began to clamber up the two hundred stone steps that led to their home. The wind howled. Waves crashed against the rocks. Lightning streaked across the sky.

"I am almost the same age as you were when you cried for your first soul," Síofra said. "And you weren't stuck on one island when you were my age! You travelled with Mamó!" Síofra was referring to her grandmother whom she loved with all her heart, using the Irish word for Granny. She was one of the oldest banshees in Ireland. She lived on an island off the west coast. Just thinking of her large gummy smile, her crinkly eyes and her bright yellow headscarf made Síofra smile.

"True. I was lucky to have your grandmother," said Silver. "Being her daughter meant that I got to travel to the banshee islands and take part in the crying ceremonies. However, it also meant that I had to grow up fast. A lot was expected of me and of your mother. She was away so much of the time and we couldn't travel with her very often."

Síofra had never thought of her mother and Aunt Silver having a demanding life.

She placed a hand on Silver's arm. "It must have been hard for you and Mother with Mamó away so often."

"Oh, Síofra, it was. Don't be in such a hurry to grow up, child."

Síofra shrugged and followed Silver inside the

wooden house. A turf fire blew puffs of smoke into the air. Silver took off her enchanted cloak and hung it on a hook on the back of the door. Then she picked up a clay pipe. She lit it from the flames of the fire and sat down on a blue rocking chair.

Síofra knelt beside her. "I'm longing so much to be a banshee, Aunt Silver. I'll be able to help you more with all the souls that drift here."

A small smile flickered like starlight on the banshee's lips. "But you'll have your own island then, Síofra, and your own souls to take care of."

Síofra stood up and walked across the room. She looked at herself in a heart-shaped mirror that hung on the wall. "My hair is as white as yours now, Silver. I long to go to the real world. To cry for the dying."

"But you must first find your cry, Síofra. You know that. But, tell me, why are you suddenly so anxious to become a banshee?" Silver stood up and walked over to her niece.

Tears sprang from Síofra's eyes. "I don't have any friends here on this island. Why don't we move to the mainland?"

"Becoming a banshee will not make you friends with the living, Síofra. In my experience, people will hate you for taking their loved ones from them."

"Can't I go to the mainland, Silver, at least until I find my cry? That way I can be around people my own age."

"One day you will leave this island, Síofra. You will find your own way. You will cry for the dying and have an island of your own to care for."

"I don't want an island of my own. I don't want to cry for the dying. I want to laugh and dance and have fun with the living."

Hot, angry tears gathered in her eyes.

"That is not the path for you, Síofra. There is a sacred path that you must follow. Once you accept that then you will never be lonely again, I promise."

Síofra flashed an angry look at Silver. "I won't accept it. I never asked to be a banshee. I don't care about the dying."

Silver gasped.

As soon as Síofra said the words she wanted to take them back. She did not hate the dying. She loved them with all her heart. Yet she wanted to meet people when they were still living. She longed to have interesting conversations, and dance with them beneath star-filled skies. She longed to go to school and learn different languages. To feel as though she belonged. How could she explain to Silver that she felt as though she was tangled in a spider's web? A web that was attached to the mainland. She longed to be close to the girl with jet-black hair. The girl who grew feathers instead of an arm. It felt as though they were linked somehow. She knew that the girl was calling her and she would stop at nothing to answer her call.

Chapter four

THE SPECTACULAR LIBRARY
OF MAGICAL THINGS

"Come with me, Síofra. It is time to show you. It is time you knew the truth."

Síofra couldn't believe it. She knew what Silver meant. She was about to enter the Spectacular Library of Magical Things.

She followed Silver up a spiral staircase that coiled its way up inside the body of the wooden dragon that clung to the outside of the house. At the top of the stairs was a magical blue door hidden by a trailing foxglove plant, an ancient plant that is poisonous to humans and harmless to banshees. A flock of one-eyed magpies flew through the air. A single white feather fell from one of the magpie's wings and landed in Síofra's hand.

"That is the magpie's way of saying that it approves of your presence here," Silver explained.

"What would happen if the magpies didn't approve of me?"

"They would peck your eyes out, of course," Silver explained as though it was the most obvious thing in the world.

For years Síofra had dreamt of setting foot in the magical library. It was a terrific and dangerous place which contained the essence of souls that were good and bad. For years she had stood at the bottom of the staircase, listening to the strange sounds and smelling the pungent odours that the blue door emitted.

Her legs trembled in anticipation. Then she gasped as Silver held her hands in the air and uttered the words:

"Objects, objects from everywhere,

Show yourselves if you dare.

The banshee has spoken,

Her words have been said.

Do not disappoint me

I have spoken to your dead."

A gust of wind gathered force and Síofra had to hold onto the bannister to avoid being flung down the stairs. Within seconds she was horizontal with her two legs stretched out behind her.

"Help me, Silver!" she screamed.

"Hold on, Síofra!" Silver's voice boomed over the sound of the wind.

Silver stepped forward and took her banshee's comb and thrust it against the door. As if by magic the gold handle on the blue door turned. The door swung open and both Silver and Síofra were blown inside by a turbulent gust of wind.

The door snapped shut behind them.

"This Spectacular Library of Magical Things contains some of the oldest books in the world," said Silver. "It is also home to the objects that belonged to every soul that ever set foot on Banshee Island. Your banshee's comb is the key that will open it."

Síofra felt dizzy as the entire room spun like a piece of thread in a spinning wheel. An assortment of smells wrestled with her nostrils.

"Here, put these on – they will help you. It can take a while to adjust to the curious atmosphere in here." Silver handed Síofra a pair of black-rimmed spectacles.

Síofra perched them on the tip of her nose and peered through them. Everything immediately appeared clearer. She looked up and above their heads was starlight. They were drifting through space.

"What is happening?"

"Don't question anything in here, Síofra. The sooner you accept things just as they are, the quicker you will adjust."

"This must be how the souls feel when they first arrive on Banshee Island!" she called to Silver as she floated in the air.

Silver was peering through her green glass bottle.

Síofra was surrounded by the most enchanted and curious objects that she had ever seen. There was a fossilised dinosaur egg, a pair of bagpipes, a medicine bottle, a diary, a doll's house, a silver locket, a ship's anchor, a medal and a baby's shoe. There were hundreds of magical objects stacked on tall shelves.

"All of these books and objects meant something to the people who owned them. The objects become magical as soon as they reach our shore. I am the guardian of this magical library. Every object has a story to tell. As a banshee, I have to record each and every one."

"There must be thousands of objects here."

"Yes, Síofra, and more arrive each day. Pick one from a shelf. Then put it to your ear."

Objects shouted at her from the shelves. "Pick me, pick me!" they cried.

A curious object caught her eye – a plant.

"Be careful with that one – it can bite!" Silver bellowed.

Síofra heeded Silver's warning as she carefully lifted the plant from the bookshelf. It was shaped like a large pitcher or a strange-looking cup. Large leafy tendrils clung to the shelf. The outside of the plant was bright-red. However, when Síofra looked inside the plant, she was so shocked at what she saw that she almost dropped the plant to the floor. The interior of the plant was lime-green in colour. There was a row of short, sharp teeth and there in a tiny plant graveyard were the carcasses of a drowned mouse and lizard. Síofra bravely held the plant close to her left ear. Not too close for fear that it would nibble on her earlobe.

Silver hushed all of the objects, like a conductor silencing an orchestra.

Then Síofra heard what the plant had to say.

"I am a carnivorous plant. I eat small animals such as frogs, lizards and small birds. I come from Mount Kinabalu, the highest mountain in Malaysia. My owner was a great explorer who had embarked on a tour of Ireland. He was giving a talk on the most unusual plants in the world, of which I am one. Two days later, as he was watching dolphins in Dingle, he had a heart attack and died. Leaving me to spend the rest of my days in this magical library."

Síofra carefully placed the pitcher-plant back onto the shelf and floated back down to the floor. How awful for this amazing plant to be so far from its mountain home, she thought.

Silver was waiting for her with a huge grin on her face.

"Well, what do you think? Isn't it spectacular?"

"Yes, it really is."

"Wait until you hear the story that the giant octopus has to tell!"

Síofra truly could not wait.

"I don't understand why you have never let me come into the library before!"

"You were not ready before now, Síofra. Do you see that dark corner over there?"

Síofra followed Silver's gaze to a dark and smelly place on the far side of the room. A swamp-like substance oozed off the library shelves. Flies buzzed overhead.

A shiver wriggled up her spine.

"There are objects there that belonged to the Booley Girls," said Silver.

"The Booley Girls? Who were they?"

"The Booley Girls were a group of young girls who vanished one evening from a mountainside in County

Wexford. One of the girls came from Soul Shadow Manor – the house across the water."

"Where did they go to?"

"They are lost in the Mists of Time. Which is a dreadful place to get lost. This dark corner appeared on the night that they disappeared."

Síofra squinted and tried to make out the objects in the dark corner of the library. However, all she could see were shadowy shapes. A strange melody drifted through the air.

"How do you know that these objects belonged to them?"

"I can see them in my green bottle. Here, see for yourself."

She thrust the green bottle at Síofra.

Excitement swam through Síofra's veins. Silver had never allowed her to peer into her green bottle before. She placed the bottle up to her right eye and gasped in astonishment. There at the end of the bottle was a vision of seven young girls, wandering around a mountainside. It was then that she spotted her. A girl with black hair. She resembled the girl she saw on the shore so much that she realised they must have been related.

"These girls appeared in my bottle on the same

45

night as the dark corner slithered into the Spectacular Library of Magical Things. It was the same night that the girl called Róisín arrived on the island. Síofra, it does not bear thinking about what would happen if the objects in the dark corner of the library got into the wrong hands. The Curse of the Booley Girls has taken up residence in that dark corner. That is why I have prevented you from coming here before. I did not want anything to happen to you. Even the good objects, such as the plant you just met, have the power to harm."

"I understand, Aunt Silver."

Silver sighed. "There is more. As you know, some of the animals and plants on the island seem to have become extinct. What you don't know is it began to happen the night the Booley Girls disappeared. I fear the island is also under a curse and the situation may get worse as time goes on. It may be that the only thing that could reverse the curse is if the Booley Girls were found. But all attempts have failed."

Síofra was horrified. "We must do something!"

"No, Síofra. The banshees have appointed others to try to recover the girls. Our job is to stay here and take care of the island." She stroked Síofra's head. "And I know you do that well because you are my niece and you will make a great banshee."

Síofra smiled. "I hope so, Aunt Silver."

"You *will*. There is something else I must show you before we leave this place."

"What is it?"

Silver walked over to a towering bookshelf. There was a tall hatbox on it. She took it off the shelf and opened it. Inside was a leather-bound book.

"This book is one of many, as you know."

Síofra recognised it straight away. It was one of *The Books of Wandering Souls*, ancient books contained the names of all the souls who had passed through Banshee Island on their way to the afterlife. Síofra had even helped Silver to write the names in the book, back in their home. It was one of the most important jobs a young banshee could do.

"What do you want to show me, Aunt Silver? I thought I already knew everything there is to know about the *Books of Wandering Souls*?"

"No, Síofra. You do not know everything."

Síofra noticed that Silver was biting her bottom lip. She only did this when she was sad.

"What is it, Aunt Silver?"

"Look – your mother wrote this. She used to record the names of the souls too. I sometimes take this book down just to look at her handwriting."

47

She pointed to some names written in a perfect flowing script.

"Oh, how wonderful!" said Síofra.

Silver sighed. "Yes, but there is something that you must know, Síofra. I had hoped I wouldn't have to tell you this until you were much older. However, it is time you knew. Maybe then you will understand why I don't want you to go to the Land of the Living."

"It would be different for me on the Land of the Living, Aunt Silver. You said so yourself. I am not a banshee. Not yet. At least not until I find my cry and attend the crying ceremony. Let me go to the mainland, Aunt Silver, just until All Hallows Eve. I will return before the island vanishes, I promise!"

Silver put the book in the hatbox and placed it on the shelf. Then she turned to face Síofra.

"Síofra ... I should have told you a long time ago but I was so scared of losing you. It is time you knew who your father was."

Síofra gasped. Her eyes widened in disbelief. She had spent her entire life wondering about that.

Silver whistled and a starling flew from a nest on the top of a bookshelf. The bird carried a golden key with a blue ribbon in its beak. It dropped the key into Silver's hand.

"Take the candle from the table, Síofra, and follow me."

Síofra did as she was told. She followed Silver through rows and rows of bookshelves containing strange objects. She noticed a jar with a set of teeth in it, as well as the bone from a whale's ribcage. Eventually, they arrived at a wall with a tapestry hanging over it. The tapestry was of Banshee Island. Each thread was carefully woven together to produce a remarkable scene. Silver found a small keyhole hidden beneath the tapestry. She placed the key into the lock and opened the door. She led Síofra into a small room.

Golden flowers were painted on the walls. Síofra held up the candle and gasped as she saw beautiful drawings of a girl with black hair, standing on a mountainside.

"These pictures are beautiful, Silver. Did you draw them?"

"No. Your mother drew them, Síofra."

"My mother? I didn't know that she was an artist."

"She was creative, Síofra. Just like you."

There was a painting of a beautiful mansion on the edge of the sea. Síofra recognised the mansion straight away. It was the house on the mainland. The house that the girl with the wing lived in.

"A long time ago, Síofra, long before you were born, I lived with your mother in a cottage on the edge of the sea. It was covered entirely with seashells. It was a beautiful place. Wild heather bloomed and we lived on the berries from the trees. It was a time when wolves roamed the land and people were scarce. It was a time when banshees lived close to humans."

"It sounds wonderful."

"Aye, it was, child. Until one day a man was out hunting wolves. Your mother was picking blackberries. I hid from the stranger, but he saw the flash of your mother's red cloak as she ran like a waterfall through the forest. He followed her and talked to her. Your mother thought that he was a kind man at first. He told her old folktales of witches and giants. He was handsome too but that turned out to be an illusion. He had jet-black hair and wore a suit cut from the finest green velvet. I hid in the trees and watched them as they danced together beneath a starlit sky." Silver smiled as she spoke, recalling how happy her sister was. "The stranger offered to take her to the village in his carriage. Your mother always longed to go to the village, Síofra, we both did. To be close to the living. However, your grandmother forbade it."

"Just like you are forbidding me now?"

"Yes. However, your mother was a wilful young woman and she stepped into the stranger's carriage. Though I often wondered if she did it to protect me. We didn't want anyone from the Land of the Living to know where we lived. She should never have gone with him, Síofra. I should have stopped her. I should have run home and told Mamó that my sister was in danger. Instead, I hid like a coward behind the trees. If I hadn't, your mother might still be here today."

"You don't know that, Aunt Silver."

"I do, Síofra. But, the awful truth is that the stranger was no ordinary man. He was the Green Man, the Rider of the Death Coach."

Síofra gasped. She had read folktales about the Green Man. There was a story about him in one of the books that Silver kept in the Spectacular Library of Magical Things. He was a scary creature, who lured people to their death.

"So he is real, Aunt Silver?"

"Yes, he is."

"So why does he ride the Death Coach, Aunt Silver? I thought it was our job as banshees to guide the souls of the dead to the afterlife."

"Not all the souls of the dead need the help of

banshees, Síofra. Those people who lived truly wicked lives get onto the Death Coach with the Green Man. He lures them to their death. Then he takes them on a journey through the Mists of Time."

A shiver darted up Síofra's spine as she thought of her mother stepping into his carriage on that warm summer's day.

"I don't understand why he would take Mother. You told me that she was a good, kind person. And what about the Booley Girls – were they bad too?"

"The Booley Girls were good. However, the Green Man used the Booley Girls to put a dreadful curse on the land and to strike fear into the hearts of the people living in the villages around the mountainside. It will stay with them for generations to come. They dread the Curse of the Booley Girls. As for your mother, she was kind and caring."

Síofra noticed how Silver used the past tense when she spoke of her mother. It was as though she was gone forever.

"The Green Man wants to stop Banshees from helping the souls of good people. The only way that he could do it was to capture a banshee and put her under his spell. Your mother was the most powerful banshee of all."

"The Green Man took Mother away?"

"Yes, Síofra. They were married the following spring in a church on the mountainside."

Síofra's heart hammered in her chest. "Married? Are you saying the Green Man, the Rider of the Death Coach, is my father?" The words lodged like stones in Síofra's throat.

"Yes, my love."

What? Her father was a monster from the pages of a fairy tale? She had always wanted to know who her father was. She had hoped that one day she could meet him. When she was younger, she imagined that he was a merman living in the depths of the ocean. She had always adored the sea. At night she lay in her bed and imagined a kingdom under the ocean that she would rule over one day.

"Oh, how horrible!" Síofra placed her hand against Silver's cheek. "And how awful for you!"

"Yes, it was, Síofra. However, I have many happy memories of your mother before she was taken from me."

Silver walked over to a large wooden wardrobe that loomed at the back of the room. She opened the doors and took out a beautiful green dress. It was embroidered with golden flowers and looked like it was made from a meadow itself.

"This was your mother's wedding dress, Síofra."

"Her wedding dress!" Tears sprang from Síofra's eyes. "But how did you get it and rescue me?"

"It was Mamó who did it. She crept into the Green Man's house one night as the clock struck midnight. You lay sleeping in your crib. Mamó snatched you. It was a cold night so she wrapped you in the only thing that she could find, your mother's green wedding dress."

"But why didn't Mamó save Mother?"

"Oh, Síofra she wanted to. Truly she did. However, your mother was too far under the Green Man's spell. He had mesmerised her. They would have both attacked Mamó. She decided to save you from a life of misery. When your mother discovered that you were taken, people heard her cry for miles around. They knew then that she was a banshee. Desperate to make their escape, your mother and the Green Man climbed into the Death Coach, and they have not been seen since. Your grandmother brought us here to this island all those years ago, to keep us safe. She was scared that the Green Man would strike again and take you back."

Síofra shuddered. "Thank you, Aunt Silver, for protecting me from such a terrible fate."

"A terrible fate indeed. But, strangely, on the Land of the Living some people even celebrate the Green Man."

"Why would they celebrate such a wicked creature?"

"They have done it since ancient times. Once a year, they hold the Green Man Festival. Girls dress in green dresses. The boys wear straw hats and they dance around a huge fire."

"How extraordinary!"

"There is something else I want to show you."

Silver pulled out a red box from the back of the wardrobe. She took off the lid and pulled out a portrait in a frame.

"It is a painting of your parents on their wedding day."

Síofra could not believe her eyes. Her mother was enthralling. She wore a bright-green wedding dress. The groom, Síofra's father, wore a matching suit. He had a pointy chin. His face reminded Síofra of an upside-down triangle. His skin looked as though it was made of leather. A small beard sprang from his chin. He reminded Síofra of a goat. When she looked down at his feet, she let out a scream.

"His feet are hooves!" she gasped.

"Yes, Síofra."

Instinctively Síofra looked down at her own feet and was grateful that she had not inherited hooves.

The couple stood arm in arm outside a splendid

house. There were other people there too. Family and friends and servants from the house. All of them wore straw hats. They were dressed for the festival. The Green Man's eyes shone like emeralds. Síofra suddenly realised that he had the same eyes as her. However, there was something else that caught her eye. She could not believe it. The painting was of the house on the mainland. Where she'd seen the young girl.

Silver read Síofra's mind. "The little girl you have seen on the shore – she lives in the house that your parents stayed in."

"Could she be related to me somehow?"

"No, Síofra, it's not possible. The Green Man was a friend of the family, that is all."

"Didn't people realise that the Green Man was wicked?"

"No, they didn't. He could be very charming, Síofra. He arrived one dark and stormy night. People were astonished. For years they had prayed that the Green Man would visit them."

"How odd!"

"Yes, many people have Green Man statues in their homes. The day he arrived they had a great celebration. He told them stories of his travels to the far-flung corners of the earth. He performed magic for them.

The people idolised him. They didn't suspect him of being wicked until the night the Booley Girls disappeared." Silver gripped Síofra's hand tightly. Her shoulders shuddered. "You must not go near the girl, Síofra. No matter how much you want to. I forbid it."

Anger bloomed like a rose in Síofra's belly. "That is not fair. You have just told me that my father was the Green Man and that he steals people's souls. You should never have left Mother with him. If she is out there somewhere then I must go and rescue her!"

"No, Síofra, you can't, it is not possible. Anyway, they haven't been seen for years. Mamó thinks that they have gone back through the Mists of Time and if you get stuck in them, you are trapped forever. You cannot escape."

A rotten thought grew like a seed in Síofra's mind.

"You must hate me, Silver. My father is a monster. You blame him for burdening you with me. If it wasn't for me you could have had an easy life."

"No, Síofra, that is not it. You are the best thing that ever happened to me."

Síofra's heart thumped in her chest. It was all starting to make sense now.

"You said it yourself. My father is wicked."

"Your mother was kind and true. You are like her in every way."

Síofra's lip trembled. Thoughts tumbled through her brain like a whirlwind. Silver had ruined her mother's life. Why didn't she stop her from going with the Green Man? She must have secretly hated her. It was all Silver's fault.

Síofra ran out of the small room and through the Spectacular Library of Magical Things. She flung the spectacles that Silver gave to her on the floor and ran down the spiral staircase as fast as her legs could carry her.

"Come back, Síofra!"

"No! I don't trust you anymore. It is all your fault that Mother isn't here. You should have stopped her!"

Síofra ran outside and Silver followed her.

The shape of a man and woman drifted towards them. There was a blue light glowing around them.

"New arrivals, Síofra. We must greet them."

Síofra stared at Silver in disbelief. She had kept this terrible secret from her all her life. She needed time to think about things and to work out a way to get into the Mists of Time and save her mother.

"I can't!"

Síofra ran as fast as she could through the Forest of

Lost Souls. Her heart thumped in her chest. She stood beneath the shelter of the trees and stared at the star-filled sky. Sometime later a golden swan flew overhead. It carried two more souls on its back. She heard Silver cry out into the darkness. It was as though she was saying farewell to old friends. Síofra never knew how long the souls would stay on the Island. It could be for a few seconds or it could be for centuries.

She walked towards the seashore. In the distance, she could see the silhouette of Soul Shadow Manor. It belonged to the girl with the wing.

"Cara, come to me! I am waiting for you!" Síofra whispered and her words drifted through the night sky, across the inky black waves and into the ear of a girl who was fast asleep in her bed.

Chapter Five

JOURNEY TO THE BANSHEE ISLAND

The grandfather clock struck midnight as Cara woke from her sleep and dreams about the Booley Girls. She shook the sleep from her wing. Then she darted from her bed over to the balcony. Banshee Island loomed closer than ever before. Cara thrust the balcony doors open and stepped outside. A gust of wind filled her lungs. Moonlight shimmered on the inky waves.

She could hear her name whispered on the breeze *"Cara, come to me! I am waiting for you!"* The banshee was calling her.

Cara knew that morning was only hours away. It was now or never. She ran back into her bedroom and picked up her red cape which hung on a silver hook on the back of her door. She reached under her bed and found her black boots. When she had put them on, she darted out of the room and out onto the landing. Her heart pounded in her ribcage. The old house creaked and moaned. It was as though it was warning her not to go. However, Cara was determined. She hurried down the marble staircase. The portraits on the wall glared down at her and she had to swallow down her fear like a boiled sweet. Once outside, she ran down the driveway as fast as her legs could carry her. She slowed down momentarily as she walked past Mr Crook's gate lodge. Cara imagined the cantankerous old man fast asleep in his bed. Snoring like a pig.

Suddenly a sound startled her. She turned her head and saw Storm, Mr Crook's pet raven, flying right at her. She covered her mouth with her hand to stifle a scream. Then she ran to the small dock where Mr Crook's little green fishing boat was moored. Storm screeched at her. Then he flew onto the side of the boat.

"Keep your voice down, Storm. If Mr Crooks hears he will have my guts for garters."

Cara carefully untied a rope that secured the boat to the dock. She jumped in and pushed against the wooden dock to shove the boat out into the water. Her heart pounded like a drum in her chest. There was a sail but she wouldn't be able to hoist it or sail with only one hand. There were oars too, luckily. Her feathers trembled as she picked up an oar and began to row further into the glistening waves. Because she couldn't hold the other oar with her wing, she had to change the oar to the other side of the boat every so often and proceed in a zig-zag fashion, just like her father had taught her to. Father told her that there was nothing that she couldn't do if she put her mind to it. His words swam through her mind.

"My darling Cara, even a bird with one wing can fly."

Cara did not understand what he meant. "No, Father, you are wrong. A bird with one wing is useless."

"You may have to struggle more than other children but one day you will soar through the clouds, believe me – and believe in yourself. But, for now, let me show you how you can row. "

And he did.

The wind howled and the waves crashed against the side of the small green boat. Cara screamed as she heard the voice of a man calling her from the shore. She looked back and saw Mr Crooks shaking his fist. He wore a straw mask over his face. He was a terrifying sight.

"Come back, you little thief! Your father will hear all about this, mark my words, Bird Girl! As for you, Storm, you are an ungrateful wretch! I will cook you for my supper tomorrow, you'll see!"

Tears sprang from Cara's eyes as she put more and more distance between herself and the angry old man on the shore. Sea mist rose from the depths of the ocean until the boat was surrounded entirely by yellow fog.

"What is happening?" Cara cried.

She had read many accounts of living people who tried to reach Banshee Island and all failed. They said that as the island became closer it simply vanished into thin air but she had never heard of it being swallowed up by mist.

"Fly on ahead, Storm, and see if you can see land."

The old bird did exactly what he was told. He flapped his wings furiously. It was as though he had made this journey many times before. The raggedy old bird seemed to know exactly what to do. He beat his wings and disappeared like a shooting star into the mist, which was turning blue.

Cara hoped that with every tug of the oars she was getting closer to Banshee Island and the girl who lived there. Moments later thunderclaps stirred the petulant murky clouds like a witch stirs a cauldron. Without any warning, the waves formed a giant's fist and tossed Cara's boat up into the air.

Cara screamed. She tried with all her might to hold on to the oar. However, with only one hand it was no use. Her outstretched wing braced itself like a small, white sail. However, it was useless against a storm of such magnitude. Cara and the small green fishing boat were no match for the magic that lay in the water surrounding Banshee Island.

Within moments Cara was sinking into the belly of the sea. However, she was not going to give up without a fight. She swam back up to the surface and gasped for air. The stars shone down from overhead. She could see the island. It was within reach. Yet the harder she tried to swim towards it, the further away it went.

It was then that she saw the young banshee. She was standing on the shore. Her white hair glistened in the moonlight.

Cara flapped her wing above the waves in desperation. *"Help me!"* she cried. Then she disappeared beneath the waves once more.

Síofra could hardly believe her eyes as she gazed through her spyglass. There in front of her, wrestling with the waves, was the girl from the mansion. She recalled Aunt Silver's words. *"You must not go near the girl, Síofra. No matter how much you want to. I forbid it."* Síofra had wanted to keep the promise that she made to her aunt. However, the girl needed her help.

Síofra had been given the task of guiding the souls of the dead, not helping the living. Yet she could not stand by and watch the girl drown when she could easily save her. She pulled off her boots and leather satchel and ran into the sea.

Chapter six

DARK AND SCARY FOLKTALES
FROM LONG AGO

"I am coming for you!" Síofra cried. Then she swam like a lightning bolt through the sea. The waves settled immediately. The magical sea was there to protect the banshee. It would never do anything to harm her.

"Help me!" Cara screamed, and then she disappeared beneath the murky waves once more. The weight of the water in her wing was pulling her under.

Síofra pulled Cara to the surface, then placed one hand behind Cara's back and another under her chin. *"Don't worry! I am here!"* she cried.

Cara gasped for air as she re-emerged like a mermaid from the sea. Her wing floated on the waves as Síofra gently guided her back to the shore.

"You're safe now," Síofra whispered into Cara's ear.

She laid her on the golden sand. The moon shone down like a silver coin.

Cara coughed loudly. "Where am I?" she gasped.

"You're on Banshee Island."

"I made it!" A small smile erupted on Cara's lips, and then she spluttered and spat up some seawater. Sitting up, she shook the water from her wing, spraying Síofra with it in the process.

There was no sign of Storm. She hoped he had not returned to wicked Mr Crooks.

Síofra smiled. She had never been so close to a living person before. She pulled on her boots and slung her satchel over her shoulder.

"Are you the banshee?" Cara asked. "You're very young."

"No. My aunt is the banshee of this island. I'm not a banshee yet – but I will be soon."

"You're not anything like what I imagined a banshee would be. Not scary at all."

Síofra laughed. "Sorry to disappoint you!"

Cara shivered. "Am I dead?"

"No, you are very much alive. However, you won't be for very much longer if you don't get a hot drink and some dry clothes. Are you able to walk?"

"I think so."

However, as she stood up her legs felt like jelly and her wing was so heavy. She stumbled and fell into Síofra's arms. She wrapped her wing around Síofra to steady herself.

"We need to hurry – here let me help you." Síofra realised that she would have to get Cara to safety. The magical island was sleeping now. However, it would wake up as soon as the sun rose. Síofra did not know what magic it would use to send Cara away and she did not want to wait to find out.

"Where are you taking me?" Cara asked.

"To my grandmother's cottage."

Cara shivered then she turned to face Síofra. She had never seen anyone like her before. Her white hair reminded her of an ice-capped mountain. Her large blue eyes shone like sapphires. If this girl was a banshee, that meant her grandmother would be too and she might not be friendly.

"What is your name?"

"My name is Síofra."

Cara smiled to herself. What a perfect name for this magical girl! In Irish it was the word for elf or sprite.

"And you are?"

"My name is Cara. It means friend in Irish."

Síofra smiled. "I know."

"Is it true what they say about your aunt, Síofra?"

"What do they say?"

"They say that she guides the souls of the dead west with the setting sun."

"Would you be my friend if I said that it was true?"

Cara stopped walking and looked into Síofra's eyes.

"Your friend?"

Cara thought of how the people of the village whispered when she was in earshot. "What kind of child is she? It's not natural. I heard her mother was a bird herself. A wild swan." Others would taunt, "She must have bewitched the girl's father. Put a spell on him."

Cara sighed.

"Forget I said anything," said Síofra. "Of course you wouldn't want to be friends with a banshee."

"You misunderstand me, Síofra. I would be honoured to be your friend. It's just that I have never had a friend before."

Síofra could not believe what she was hearing. Cara lived in a beautiful mansion in the Land of the Living – how could she not have any friends?

Cara's long black hair framed her face. Two green eyes stared back at Síofra. Her wing hung from her shoulder. The feathers brushed off the ground. She was truly magnificent.

"I don't understand," Síofra said.

"You must think that I'm very strange, Síofra. I have tried to make friends with other children in the town where I live. But they just laugh at me and call me 'Bird Girl'. They think I am cursed. That my mother was a wicked swan who put a spell on my father."

"So people can be cruel."

"Yes, they can."

"Well, I think you're wonderful, Cara."

Cara smiled. No one had ever called her wonderful before.

"Have you ever heard of the Booley Girls, Síofra?"

"My Aunt Silver has told me about them. She said that they vanished without a trace from a mountainside thirty years ago."

"Kitty, my housemaid, told me that one of the Booley Girls was my aunt."

"Really!"

"Yes. My grandmother lives with us but she has never got over losing her daughter. She stays in bed all day long crying."

"I am sorry to hear that, Cara. Truly I am. Didn't the Booley girls disappear on the night of the summer solstice?"

"That's right. During the Green Man Festival."

A shiver darted up Síofra's spine like a lightning bolt.

"You don't celebrate the Green Man, do you, Cara?"

Cara shook her head. "It's just a harmless bit of fun really, Síofra. A pagan feast from ancient times. Our ancestors celebrated it. Then when the Booley Girls went missing, people suspected that the Green Man took them so they live in fear of him now. We still have the festival each year in case he comes back again."

Síofra frowned. Silver was right. The people on the mainland did live in fear of the Green Man.

"And Kitty said to me that people are scared of the curse of the Booley Girls too. Many believe that they haunt the mountainside."

"What do you believe, Cara?"

"I don't believe any of it," said Cara, not wanting Síofra to think she was foolish enough to believe in it. "Although we do have a painting of the Green Man and his wife in our house. Father won't let us take it down. He said that if we do it will bring bad luck."

"How could it? It's only a painting."

"Some say that the Green Man is married to the banshee." Cara clasped her hands over her lips as soon as she uttered the words. All this time she had been speaking and she had completely forgotten that Síofra

71

was a banshee. "Oh, I'm sorry, Síofra. I didn't mean to be so insensitive. Father always says that I should think before I open my mouth."

Síofra felt her neck flush. She didn't want to talk about this with Cara. She hardly knew her and she hadn't come to terms with the fact that a man with hooves for feet was her father.

"Do you go to the Green Man Festival, Cara?"

"Yes, everyone does. It's a chance for people to get dressed up. Although I must admit that some people take it too far. They knock on people's doors and scare them with their masks. Then there's the hunt, of course."

"The hunt?"

"Yes, according to local custom each year on the summer solstice the youngest person at the festival is blindfolded, and then they are spun around three times. After that, they must walk through the crowd of people and select someone to be hunted."

"Hunted? Like an animal?"

Cara plucked one of the feathers from her wing, as she often did when she felt anxious. "Yes. It sounds ridiculous when I say it out loud."

"Why on earth would they hunt a person?"

"They believe that if they don't hunt someone the

Green Man will rise again. He will come for others. More people will disappear, just like the Booley Girls did all those years ago."

"It sounds like nonsense to me." But, in fact, she was very disturbed by what Cara was telling her.

"Yes, Síofra, it is."

"What happens if a person objects to being hunted?"

"They get hunted anyway. They don't have a choice in the matter."

A thought crossed Síofra's mind like a bird across a cloudless sky. "Do you think that the Green Man himself had anything to do with the disappearance of the Booley Girls?"

Cara noticed that Síofra seemed to believe in the Green Man after all. "Kitty my maid thinks so. She said that the Green Man rides the Death Coach. That he came for those girls like a bird goes for a worm. Many believe that he will come again."

"What about you, Cara? What do you believe?"

"I know it must sound strange to you, Síofra, but I have never questioned it before. The Green Man Festival and the hunt were around before I was born."

Síofra frowned. There was so much about the Land of the Living that she did not know. So much that Silver hadn't told her.

"Everything seems strange to me, Cara. I have never left Banshee Island."

Cara felt sorry for Síofra. She had missed out on so many things. Things that she had taken for granted, like going to school and travelling to other countries. She reached out her wing and stroked Síofra's face with the tip of her feathers.

"Up until now, I believed that girls with wings only existed in fairy tales," said Síofra. "I have a book which tells about them."

"I have never met anyone else like me, Síofra. But there *are* others out there like me. I know it." A shiver danced up her feathers as she spoke.

A thought struck Síofra. "You said that one of the Booley Girls was your aunt, Cara. What was her name?"

"It was Róisín."

The girl who came to the island, Síofra thought. How extraordinary! This was fate indeed. But she wouldn't tell Cara yet.

"Do you know much about her, Cara?"

"Kitty told me that she was the seventh daughter of a seventh daughter, which gave her certain powers."

"Oh, yes, that is true. Aunt Silver told me so."

"She had the power to heal any illness. People would travel for days just to see her. The mountain folk believe that her ghost haunts my family. But I don't believe that she is dead. I feel as though she is still alive. Does that make sense to you?"

"Yes, Cara. It makes perfect sense. My mother vanished too. Silver told me that the Green Man took her. I intend to find her and bring her home."

"Really? How terrible! So you actually do believe in the Green Man, Síofra?"

Síofra didn't answer. "We are nearly there," she said.

She led Cara through the starlit forest. Fireflies danced in the air. A hill carpeted in golden buttercups emerged before them. In the centre of the hill was a green wooden door. The hill looked like the belly of a giant. A bubbling stream wound itself around the hill like a scarf. The branches of a large hawthorn tree loomed overhead. They clawed at the night's sky like the fingers of giants.

"This is my grandmother's old house."

Cara gripped Síofra's wrist. "Wait."

"What is it?"

"What if your grandmother doesn't want me here?"

"There is no need to be frightened, Cara. She isn't here anymore. But, in any case, she wouldn't hurt you. She would love you – and you would love her!"

"Where does your grandmother live now?"

"Her home is on an island with an ancient lighthouse off the West Coast of Ireland. She stays in this cottage when she comes to visit."

"Don't you miss her?"

"Yes, I do. She is a very important banshee. She goes to great battles to lead the dead to the otherworld."

Cara's heart sank like a stone. She recalled the battle that was about to take place back home in Enniscorthy. If only there was some way that she could stop it.

Suddenly a fox cub bounded through the forest and jumped into Síofra's arms. It nuzzled its head against her cheek.

"Niamh! I wondered where you were. Niamh, meet Cara."

"She's beautiful!"

"The real Niamh died many years ago, Cara. This is her ghost."

Cara reached out and stroked the small animal. Her fur felt warm beneath her fingers. She felt very much alive.

Síofra looked up at the sky. It had turned a dusty-pink colour. The sun would rise soon. She watched the swans flying through the sky, bringing the latest souls to the afterlife.

"We need to get inside right away, Cara. It's not safe for you out here."

Síofra placed Niamh on the grass. Then she reached around her neck, where the key to her grandmother's house hung on a length of gold ribbon. She took it off and opened the wooden door. Then she went inside, Niamh at her heels.

Cara gasped as she stepped into the house in the hill. It was much larger than it had looked from outside.

Síofra walked over to the fireplace and clicked her fingers. Immediately a roaring fire blazed on the hearth. There was a washing line strung across the centre of the room laden with dresses, shirts, trousers and coats, oddly all in different sizes. In every nook and cranny, there were stacks of books piled high.

The floor of the cottage was made of glass. Cara looked down and saw a river flowing beneath it. Then she gasped as the largest salmon she had ever seen swam beneath them. It was as big as a horse.

"Síofra, that fish reminds me of the Salmon of Knowledge."

"That's because it is a Salmon of Knowledge," Síofra said as though it was the most obvious thing in the world.

"It can't be the actual Salmon of Knowledge." Cara could hardly believe her ears. She had heard stories about the magical salmon. "In the legend, they say that Fionn ate the salmon and he gained all the knowledge in the world."

"Yes, he did. However, there was more than one Salmon of Knowledge. It would be foolish to just have one."

It never occurred to Cara that there could be more than one.

"Come pick a dress from the washing line, Cara – there must be one to fit you."

Cara reached up and picked a red-velvet dress with a satin bow.

"This could work. Does your grandmother own a pair of scissors, Síofra?"

Síofra walked over to an old kitchen dresser. She opened the drawer and pulled out a large pair of scissors with golden handles and handed them to Cara. Síofra watched as Cara carefully snipped a sleeve off the dress to make room for her wing. Then she took off her wet cape and nightdress and stepped into the dress. Her wing bloomed like a flower through the hole that she had cut for it.

"Your wing is beautiful, Cara. " Síofra's eyes opened in amazement at the sight of it.

"I don't usually show it to people. I try to keep it covered most of the time."

"Why would you hide your beauty from the world?"

Síofra ran her fingers along Cara's feathers.

Cara smiled. "You might find my wing beautiful, Síofra, but the people where I come from consider me to be a monster." She walked over to the washing line as she spoke. "Who do all these clothes belong to?"

"They belong to the dead."

Cara shuddered as she recalled stories about banshees washing the clothes of the dead in rivers and streams around Ireland.

"What does it feel like to be a banshee, Síofra?"

"I'm not sure, Cara. You see, I am not a real banshee until I find my cry. That won't happen for a while yet."

Without warning a small blue door opened on a cuckoo clock on the wall and a wooden figure with a sword in his hand ran out, chasing a man. It was almost morning.

Cara gasped. Her father would be getting up soon to prepare for the journey back to their castle in Enniscorthy. What would he do when he discovered that she had gone? Then there was Mr Crook's boat. He might have already told her father that she stole it from him. She would be in great trouble. Spellfinder would lock her in her bedroom for days. She would pluck all of her feathers out, she was sure of it.

"I have to go home, Síofra. My father will be looking for me."

"You can't leave, Cara. Don't you understand?"

"Understand what?"

"This island does everything it can to keep banshees safe from the Land of the Living. That is why it is only visible to the human eye once every seven years and it is impossible for the living to reach it."

"I got here, didn't I?"

"Yes. That was because I helped you. Otherwise, you would have drowned in the waves. If the island discovered a living soul here, I don't know what it would do."

"But maybe you can help me to leave too? My father is returning to my home town of Enniscorthy today. There is to be a great battle. Everyone in the town has to play their part. Men, women and children." Cara recalled the sad look in her father's eyes when he spoke of the battle that was to take place on Vinegar Hill.

"Many souls have arrived on this island after battles, Cara. I hate to think of you going home to that, even if you could."

"I don't have a choice but to try."

Síofra could see the sadness in Cara's eyes and she understood exactly what she meant. She too had to do what her aunt told her. She was forbidden to leave Banshee Island and was destined to a life guiding the souls of the dead.

Suddenly an idea spread like ink on a page in Cara's mind. "What if you came back with me?"

"To the Land of the Living?"

"Yes. We could be friends forever."

Síofra nibbled her bottom lip and paced up and down as she thought.

"I have always wanted to go to the Land of the Living."

Cara's heart lifted. It made perfect sense. She could leave the island under Síofra's protection. Surely she could persuade her father to give Síofra employment in the castle as a chambermaid, even if it did mean working with wicked Spellfinder. Cara would never be lonely again.

Síofra wanted to go with all her heart. But then she thought of Silver and Mamó and all that they had sacrificed for her. She could never leave them.

"I'm sorry, Cara, but I can't go with you. A banshee brings death everywhere she goes. You are risking your life just by being here with me now. I would

81

never forgive myself if you died because of me."

Síofra lowered her head in despair. Then she raised her eyes and met Cara's gaze.

"There is something else too."

"What is it, Síofra?"

"Can I trust you, Cara?"

"Yes, of course you can trust me. You are my friend. What is wrong?"

"Tonight for the first time I discovered the identity of my father."

"How exciting, Síofra! What is he like?"

"Not what I expected, Cara."

"Oh, is he tall and handsome? Or a pirate, sailing on the Seven Seas!"

"That's the thing, Cara. My father is a wicked man. I am terrified that I will turn out just like him."

Cara gasped as she suddenly recalled the painting that hung in Soul Shadow Manor. The painting of the banshee and the Green Man on their wedding day.

"The Green Man!" she gasped.

"Yes." Síofra hung her head.

Cara had always hated the painting. The Green Man had hooves for feet and whenever you walked past the painting his beady green eyes stared at you. What a terrible thing to discover!

She walked over to Síofra and wrapped her wing around her.

"You could never be wicked, Síofra. You have just saved my life. I wouldn't be here if it wasn't for you! That was the kindest thing that anyone has ever done for me."

Síofra smiled. Cara was right. Deep down she knew that she could never be a monster like her father, although Silver had told her that many people in the Land of the Living called banshees monsters.

Síofra sighed. Despite all the warnings that Silver and Mamó gave to her, she longed to experience the Land of the Living before her cry arrived. This could be her last chance. Besides, she had only just got to know Cara. She couldn't say goodbye. Not yet.

"I will go with you, Cara, but there are certain conditions."

"Yes?"

"First – I am not a full banshee yet as I haven't found my cry. However, it could arrive at any moment and if that happens then being close to people may put them at a greater risk of dying. Especially if I care for them. I care for you, Cara, so you are in danger if my cry comes. That means that I will then have to return to the Island."

"I understand."

"Secondly, when I join you on the Land of the Living I must find my mother. I need you to take me to the place where the Booley Girls were last seen."

"Oh, no, Síofra! I couldn't possibly."

"Why ever not?"

"The Booley Girls want their revenge. It is not safe on the mountains. I have told you about the curse."

"Yes, Cara, you have. That is why I need to go there. I have to help them. My aunt says they are trapped in the Mists of Time. Maybe I could rescue your Aunt Róisín as well as my mother."

"I don't see how you can find them, Síofra. Many have tried over the years, but no-one has succeeded."

"You must never give up hope, Cara. Many people have tried to reach Banshee Island over the years – they failed and yet you have succeeded."

"With your help."

"Yes. And we can be together again in this search, if you agree."

"But there is one thing that I don't understand, Síofra. Why do you care so much about the Booley Girls? I can understand why you want to find your mother but the Booley Girls are nothing to you."

"Ever since the night that the Booley Girls

disappeared some of the plants and animals living on this island have gone extinct, Cara."

"How awful!"

"It truly is. Aunt Silver fears that it could get worse as the years pass by – the island itself could die. The only way to save Banshee Island is to rescue the Booley Girls. That should reverse the curse."

"What you are suggesting is dangerous, Síofra. The Green Man won't just stand by and allow you to save your mother and the Booley Girls. He'll put up a fight. A fight that you could lose."

"It's a chance that I am willing to take."

"You are a brave girl, Síofra."

Síofra felt heat rise in her cheeks. "There is something else, Cara."

"What is it?"

"When it is time for me to return you must promise to let me go, no matter how hard it is to say goodbye. If I am not back here before the island disappears, I might never get back."

Cara bit down on her bottom lip. She knew that it would be hard to say goodbye to her new friend. However, it would be selfish of her to keep her away from Banshee Island. "Yes, I promise."

"And you must never tell anyone about me. No

matter what happens. If people find out that I am a young banshee they might hurt me or worse still they might kill me."

Cara gasped. "I could not bear anything to ever happen to you, Síofra."

A huge smile erupted like sunshine on a cloudy day on Síofra's lips.

"I think we should give each other something to seal our friendship," she said.

Cara nodded in agreement. "I would like that, Síofra."

"But I don't have much to give." Síofra reached into her leather satchel and pulled out an ancient silver comb. The Irish word *Bean-sí* was engraved on it. Two of the teeth were missing and it contained some strands of Síofra's snow-white hair. "I wish I could give you this, Cara, but it is a key to the Spectacular Library of Magical Things. Mamó gave it to Silver and Silver gave it to me. She said I must protect it at all costs."

"You love Silver, don't you?"

"Yes. She has taken care of me ever since I was a baby." Síofra felt guilt rise like smoke in a chimney. She regretted saying all those horrible things to Silver. She should never have blamed her for what happened to her mother. It was all the Green Man's fault.

Cara peered down at the ring that she wore. It had

a silver swan engraved on it.

"I want you to have this friendship ring. It will mean that we are together even when we are apart."

Cara took the ring off and handed it to Síofra. Then she hugged her tightly.

"Oh Cara. It is beautiful, but I couldn't possibly take it."

"Why ever not?"

"It is too precious."

Cara sighed." Don't worry Síofra, I have lots of rings back home in Soul Shadow Manor. Father gets a silversmith in Dublin to make jewellery for me."

"That is kind of him."

"I suppose so. Although he only does it because he feels guilty about being away so much. Anyway, I think that the ring suits you."

"Thank you, Cara." Síofra reached into her bag and pulled out a piece of blue sea glass that was shaped like a heart.

She handed it to Cara, who held it tightly in her hand.

"It is not as nice as the ring you gave me, Cara, but it is all I have apart from my comb."

Tears sprang from Cara's eyes. "It is perfect, Síofra, just like you." The piece of sea glass meant more to her than all the rings her father had given to her.

"We must go now, Cara. Before the sun has fully risen in the sky."

Niamh yelped, as if she understood.

Síofra picked up the fox cub and kissed her nose.

"I am sorry, old friend. I have to go for a while. However, I will be back as soon as I can."

Síofra's heart ached. She knew that the ghost of Niamh might leave the island while she was away. No one ever knew when that would happen. She might never see her little friend again. She wished that she could take her with her. But that was impossible. Síofra placed Niamh on Mamó's worn chair in front of the fire.

Then she ran over to some piles of books and started to search through them.

"What are you looking for?"

"A collection of ancient folktales. The book I mentioned to you before. It is called *Dark and Scary Folktales from Long Ago*. It has the story of the Green Man in it. It also has a story about children who have wings like you, Cara. This book could help us to find out who we really are and where we came from."

"Here, let me help you. What does the book look like?"

"It has a green leather cover."

"Is that it, Síofra? In that other pile?"

"Yes, that's it, Cara!"

Cara pulled the book from the pile and handed it to Síofra and, as she did, something fell from the pages and drifted onto the floor.

Síofra picked it up.

"What is it, Síofra?"

Síofra unfolded the piece of paper and studied it. On it was a beautiful watercolour painting of a musical organ that was brightly coloured and sat on four large wheels. There were four golden swans on each corner and a set of pipes for the music to escape. She handed the painting to Cara.

Cara laughed. "Oh, it's a musical street organ! I saw one once before when I was in Dublin. A man was pushing it along the streets. Father told me that the man was called an organ-grinder. As the organ-grinder pushed the organ the most beautiful music came out of the pipes. It is quite magical. There were other performers with him too. Puppeteers and storytellers. Children followed them and sang along."

"I wonder what it is doing in the pages of this book. I never noticed it before. We must go now, Cara, but I am taking this book with me – you keep the painting."

Cara put the illustration into her pocket and, as she

did so, she noticed something written on the other side. She would check that later.

Síofra picked up her brown-leather satchel and stuffed the book inside.

Síofra reached out and took Cara's hand. She smiled at her new friend. She sensed that their fates were entwined. There was no way of knowing if she could make it to the Land of the Living. Yet she wanted to rescue her mother and bring her back home and she was willing to risk everything to do it.

Chapter seven

THE WITCHES' MEADOW

Síofra and Cara ran as fast as they could through the Forest of Dead Souls. They needed to get away before the island woke up and realised that Cara was there.

"This way, Cara. I know a shortcut." Síofra knew that it was a risk to take a living girl on a shortcut through the witches' meadow. The meadow was home to a coven of wicked witches who shapeshifted into large, black hares. They had escaped to the island many moons ago when they were driven from the Land of the Living. The witches detested humans and would stop at nothing to take Cara's life. However, if the girls went back the way they came, Síofra knew that they would risk bumping into Silver who would be greeting a new arrival of souls. The anger of a banshee was not something that she wanted Cara to witness.

As soon as they set foot in the witches' meadow the weather changed. The blue sky which hung like a curtain above their heads fell to reveal a swirling grey mist. Lightning flashed above their heads. Hailstones as big as rocks fell from the sky. Cara screamed as she narrowly avoided one of the hailstones. Síofra gripped her hand tightly. Even Silver and Mamó couldn't protect them here. The witches lived side by side with the banshees on the understanding that they didn't set foot on each other's territory. The witches performed their spells and the banshees guided the souls of the dead. However, in recent years Silver had noticed some strange activity. The number of witches on the island had declined. Silver suspected that they were leaving the island somehow. Mamó had heard rumours that many had returned to the Land of the Living. The greatest coven in Ireland was in County Kilkenny.

Síofra detested the witches. "The witches would do anything to get into the Spectacular Library of Magical Things," Silver had explained. "It was the witches who robbed the swans of their song." Síofra shuddered to think what they would do if they got hold of the objects cursed by the Booley Girls in the dark corner of the library. The witches' spells would be so powerful that they could take over the world.

Síofra was determined to keep her friend safe. "Hurry, Cara. This way!" She could feel Cara's hand trembling. Her wing flapped in the breeze. Regret washed over Síofra like a waterfall. What was she thinking of, bringing her new friend to such a dangerous part of the Island? It was a stupid idea. A storm cloud of thought entered Síofra's mind: *Perhaps Silver is right. Maybe I'm not ready for the responsibility of becoming a banshee yet.*

Thunder rumbled. It was then that Síofra spotted a giant black hare standing on its hind legs, sniffing the air. The hare was as tall as a tree. Long pointy ears stretched from the animal's head. Síofra knew that this hare was one of the witches. It was not just any witch. It was Talia, the youngest and most fierce of all the witches. She must have caught Cara's scent. They had no time to lose.

She pulled Cara down behind a large rock.

"We have to wait here until the coast is clear, Cara," she whispered.

"What is that thing?" Cara asked as she gasped for breath.

"It's a witch."

"A witch!" Cara's eyes widened in horror.

Had the situation not been so treacherous Síofra would have smiled at the startled expression on Cara's face.

"Do you think she has seen us?" Cara asked.

"I don't think so. Although it's hard to tell. Hares have a strong sense of smell. They may have picked up your scent."

Cara and Síofra peered over the edge of the rock. The large black hare had been joined by three even larger hares. Their jet-black ears protruded from their bony scalps. They huddled together like bees around a flower.

"Witches shapeshift into hares, Cara," Síofra whispered.

"Just like swans can shapeshift into humans."

Cara knew of the superstition about witches turning into hares although she hadn't believed it was true until now. "I have heard of it before. Kitty, my maid, told me that a farmer shot a hare who was stealing his crops. The bullet hit the animal in the leg. The farmer followed the wounded animal to a cottage and inside he found an old woman sitting at the fireside with a gunshot wound in her leg. Kitty said the old woman was a witch."

"Kitty was right, Cara. We are not safe on this part

of the island. I wanted to avoid running into Aunt Silver by getting to the shore this way, but it was foolish of me."

Síofra and Cara stayed as still as possible and watched as the hares built a gigantic bonfire with wood from the forest. Then they danced around it, playing tambourines that were adorned with green ribbons.

"What are they doing now?"

"They are preparing for the summer solstice. Each year on the longest day of the year the witches gather. They must be starting their celebrations early."

The hares gathered up bodhráns and tin whistles and played the strangest music Cara had ever heard.

"It reminds me of the Green Man Festival," she whispered.

Síofra looked at the witches. She decided that now was as good a time as any for them to make a run for it, while the hares were distracted playing music.

"On the count of three we will run around the edge of the field and through the canopy of weeping willow trees over there – do you see them?"

Cara nodded. Her heartbeat pounded as loudly as the witches' drums.

"Wait, Síofra. What if they see us?"

"It's a chance that we have to take. We can't go back the way we came or the witches will certainly see us. Here take my hand. *One – two – three!*"

Hand in hand, they ran around the edge of the meadow and over to the sanctuary of the weeping-willow trees. At one point Cara stumbled and fell. As Síofra pulled her up, she failed to notice that the piece of blue sea glass that Síofra had given to her had fallen from her pocket.

Chapter eight

A GHOST AT THE WINDOW

The canopy of weeping-willow trees lined a stony path that led Síofra and Cara down to a beach. There was a large fishing boat waiting on the shore. More items had washed up on the beach. There was a rocking horse, a piano and a painting of a little girl in a yellow dress.

"Where did all of these objects come from?"

"They belong to the dead. They wash up on the shore before the souls arrive."

"What do you do with them?"

"Silver puts them into the Spectacular Library of Magical Things."

"They don't look magical."

"They don't gain their magic until they enter the library."

"It sounds fascinating, Síofra."

"Yes, it is. Perhaps I can take you there sometime. But come on! The witches are cunning creatures. They may follow us here. Help me to get the boat out into the water before it's too late."

Together the girls wrestled with the waves. They waded into the water, pushing the boat from the shore, then jumped on board.

They were both exhausted. Cara's wing was wet and hung limply from her shoulder blade. Síofra hoisted the sail and picked up her spyglass. In the distance, the tiny speck that was the manor house swam into view.

"I hope that we have a safe crossing, Síofra," Cara said through chattering teeth. Thoughts of her own terrifying crossing to the island were still fresh in her mind. The sky above their heads had turned blue. They had left the thunderstorm behind them in the witches' meadow. Daylight erupted on the horizon.

"I will do my very best to get you home safely, Cara," Síofra said.

Then she opened a wooden chest and pulled out a large-brimmed purple hat and a large blue overcoat with golden buttons. She put on the coat and hat. Then she grabbed the wooden wheel.

"I am Síofra, the Great Warrior Queen!" she announced as she steered the boat, as she had seen her grandmother do many times.

Cara giggled into her cupped hand. She thought that Síofra looked more like a swashbuckling pirate.

Síofra looked back at Banshee Island. She had begged her grandmother to allow her to join her on the journey to the other islands – however, the answer she got was always the same. "You are not ready yet, child. The world is a big place. When the time is right I will take you on the journey of a lifetime." Mamó would smile to reveal her gummy mouth.

Síofra was fed up with waiting for Mamó and Silver to tell her when she was old enough to do things. From now on *she* would decide where she went and what she did when she got there. She had always dreamed of being a pirate and sailing across wide blue oceans. Perhaps this was her chance.

Cara felt nervous. Her father would be looking for her by now and Mr Crooks would tell them that she stole his boat. Then there was the issue of Síofra – how on earth was she going to explain it all?

Síofra saw the worried look on Cara's face.

"There is no need to worry, Cara. The witches are back on the island."

A giant wave crashed over the edge of the fishing boat and nearly sent the girls tumbling overboard.

"It's not the witches that I am worried about, Síofra."

"What is it then?"

"We need to make up a story to tell my father about who you are and how we met. I can't tell them that you are a banshee and that I found you on the island, can I?"

"Oh, I hadn't thought about that. Of course your father will want to know where you've been all night."

"That's not all. The boat that I travelled on belonged to Mr Crooks, our grumpy old gardener. I stole it from him. He will never forgive me."

Cara looked at Síofra as she steered the boat. She had never met such a confident girl before. In fact, she didn't behave much like a girl at all, or at least not any that Cara had met before. Síofra was the most peculiar-looking girl that she had ever seen, with her hair cut in a blunt bob with a fringe and white as snow. She had a small little heart-shaped birthmark on her neck and a sprinkling of freckles across the bridge of her nose. Kitty would think that Síofra was unladylike. How could a young girl wear a waistcoat and red trousers? It was unheard of. Yet these were all the things that Cara loved about her new friend.

"We need food. It will help us to think better. Under the bench that you are sitting on, you will find a wooden box. Inside of it is my grandmother's supply of seaweed snacks."

"Seaweed snacks? That sounds disgusting, Síofra!"

"It is the tastiest food you will ever eat and good for the brain," Síofra said as she tapped her forehead.

Cara lifted the seat and found a wooden box containing seaweed. She thrust a handful of it at Síofra and sat back down.

"I have an idea already," Síofra announced, her cheeks bulging with seaweed.

"I am all ears."

"You could tell your father that you couldn't sleep so you went outside and saw me drowning in the sea. There was no time to lose so you stole Mr Crooks' fishing boat and you rescued me."

Cara sniggered as Síofra relived every aspect of their imaginary adventure, so emphatically that Cara almost believed her.

"Suddenly there was a storm and we were both thrown overboard and washed up further down the coast. Then we found an abandoned boat and sailed back."

"I don't know if they will believe it, Síofra. It all sounds a bit strange."

"Have you got any better ideas?"

Cara realised that she hadn't and the shoreline was in sight. They would reach dry land soon.

"Won't they ask where you came from?"

"Just say my father is a fisherman. He fell overboard during a storm. That's when you found me clinging to the sail of his fishing boat, mourning his loss."

"It's worth a try."

They had no choice.

Sometime after, they approached Soul Shadow Manor. Cara picked up Siofra's spyglass and focused it on some people standing on the shore. It was her father, Mr Crooks and Kitty. They had obviously sighted the boat. She was relieved to see that Spellfinder wasn't there. Butterflies danced in her ribcage as she feared that she would be in big trouble.

Soon Síofra was running the boat directly towards the shore where the group of people waited.

"Don't just stand there, man!" Cara's father shouted. *"Help me to haul them in!"*

Mr Crooks was flabbergasted. His mouth was wide open.

"Yes, sir. Of course, sir." He followed Cara's father out into the sea.

The boat reached them and they hauled it in and up onto the sandy shore.

"*Father!*" Cara cried as he lifted her out of the boat and onto the safety of the shore.

Síofra felt a pang of sadness when she saw the relief in Cara's father's eyes. He was overjoyed to see his daughter safe and well. Síofra wished with all her heart that her father was a good, kind man. Not a wicked character from an ancient folktale.

Kitty rushed forward to embrace Cara.

"Who have we here?" Cara's father asked, nodding towards Síofra.

"Father, this is my friend Síofra."

"I am very pleased to make your acquaintance, Síofra. My name is Séamus O'Leary. Can I help you out of the boat?"

"I can manage myself, thank you, sir."

"Please call me Séamus."

Síofra smiled at Séamus. He had a long handlebar moustache that twirled up at the ends and large brown eyes like a seal. He was a handsome man and Cara resembled him.

"Crooks, run back to the Manor House and tell Mrs

Spellfinder that Miss O'Leary is safe and sound and ask her to prepare an extra seat at the table for breakfast."

"What about my fishing boat? The little miss here stole it and –"

"Do as you are told, man. There will be plenty of time to discuss your blasted fishing boat later. Now is not the time for it. Do you understand me?"

"Yes, sir."

Séamus winked conspiratorially at the girls. They giggled and smiled back at him.

"Don't think that you have got away lightly, Cara. Some questions need answering. Like what you were doing out of your bed in the middle of the night? And where in the world did you find Síofra?"

"Oh, that was extraordinary, Father," said Cara and prepared to trot out their alibi.

"You can tell me later, my dear – but now let us get you back home. I will go ahead. There is much to be done before we return to Enniscorthy later today. But first I have some business to attend to back at the house."

Cara frowned at the mention of Enniscorthy.

"I will talk to you later, Cara. You need to learn that your actions have consequences."

"Yes, Father," Cara replied and her father hurried on ahead.

Síofra turned to Kitty when Mr O'Leary was out of earshot.

"Cara told me that her Aunt Róisín was one of the Booley Girls," she said.

Kitty looked Síofra up and down. What kind of a girl was she at all? Dressed in trousers like a boy and a head of white hair like an old beggar woman. Frown lines converged on Kitty's forehead.

"Cara, you promised me that you wouldn't speak about the Booley Girls again."

Cara bowed her head. "I'm sorry, Kitty."

"It's alright. You have been in enough trouble for one day. I can see that Síofra is your friend."

"Yes, she is, Kitty."

"Well, Síofra, tomorrow is the thirtieth anniversary of the girls' disappearance."

"Is the Green Man Festival still going ahead this year, Kitty?" asked Cara. "Despite the battle of Vinegar Hill and the rebellion?"

"Yes, Cara, it is. It will take place the day after tomorrow. Mr Crooks and Spellfinder have talked of nothing else. They have even made a giant version of the Green Man out of straw. It is a hideous thing. They are going to burn it in a huge bonfire on Mount Leinster."

"It sounds ghastly. But why would they burn it?" Síofra asked.

"Some sort of ancient ritual. Some people believe that the Booley Girls will appear tomorrow night as a mysterious comet has been spotted in the sky. The last time the comet appeared was when the girls disappeared."

"I am surprised Father is allowing it," said Cara.

"Your father has enough on his mind, Síofra. I don't think he knows much about it."

Síofra shielded her eyes from the sun, then she turned to face Kitty. "Cara told me that people believe that a ghost haunts her family."

"Don't say that too loud around here, Síofra. But, yes, that is what folk say."

"What about you, Kitty, do you believe in ghosts?" A shiver skipped down Síofra's spine. Róisín could be the ghost of a Booley Girl. Perhaps she was haunting the family. Silver had told her that ghosts only appear when they have some unfinished business with the living.

"I don't know what to believe, Síofra. Now come on, you two. Spellfinder will be waiting for us and you two have a lot of explaining to do."

"Spellfinder?" Síofra whispered to Cara.

"She is our housekeeper. She cared for my father since he was a boy. Stay well clear of her if you can, Síofra. She is a miserable old crow."

Síofra and Cara followed Kitty along the statue-lined drive. Carriages were drawn up before the house. The girls climbed the stone steps that led to the entrance. Síofra could not believe it. This was the house in the painting that Silver had shown her. The painting of her parents on their wedding day. She had so many questions that she wanted answers to.

Suddenly something caught her eye. A girl was looking out of a bedroom window. Síofra could not help but find it strange as Cara had told her that she was an only child. Whoever the girl was, she appeared to be crying. She was banging on the window with her fists, as if trying to get out.

"Who is that?" Síofra said, pointing to the bedroom window.

"I don't see anyone. You must be imagining it."

"A girl is standing at the third window from the left on the second floor."

Cara squinted in the sunlight and stared up at the window. However, no one was there. "I can't see anyone, Síofra. The room you're pointing at hasn't been used in years. It belonged to my Aunt Róisín when she was a girl. Grammy had it locked up ever since she vanished."

"You really can't see her? She looks like she's in great distress."

"Síofra, you are scaring me. I can't see anyone at all."

A scowl appeared on Cara's face. It had not occurred to her that being friends with a young banshee meant that the spirits of lost souls would be close by at all times. Although she was aware of Róisín's presence, she hadn't seen her before and she wanted to keep it that way.

Síofra sensed Cara's distress. So she reached out and touched her feathers.

"I am sorry, Cara. I didn't mean to scare you."

"It's alright. You can't help it if you can see spirits. Do you think the girl could be Róisín?"

"I honestly don't know." However, Síofra had the feeling that the restless spirit was in trouble and needed her help.

Chapter nine

SOUL SHADOW MANOR

"This is the most beautiful house I ever saw," Síofra said as they stepped into the elaborate entrance hall. The floor was carved from Italian marble and shone so brightly that she could see her face in it. She stuck out her tongue at her reflection and Cara laughed.

Housemaids and butlers ran around them like flocks of crows, carrying luggage out to the carriages and a small dog yapped at their ankles.

Síofra looked up at the paintings that hung alongside the staircase. She had never seen anything like them. A crystal chandelier hung from the ceiling.

"Into the dining room, the pair of you," Kitty ordered.

Síofra's stomach grumbled in reply.

Síofra followed Kitty into the dining room. A long oak table was set for breakfast. There were silver goblets and matching plates. A fire blazed in the hearth.

"You can sit next to me, Síofra," Cara said.

Síofra sat down on a wooden chair with a red velvet cushion. She pulled a silver lid off a bowl of porridge- like a magician revealing a magic trick. She was famished. She picked up the spoon and shovelled the food into her mouth. It went everywhere.

Cara smiled and then the smile fell from her lips like a shooting star from the sky when Mrs Spellfinder sauntered in. She had a face like thunder. She held a strange-looking mask made from twigs in front of her face. There were two holes for her eyes. She wore a small straw brooch, shaped like a small man, on her left shoulder. Her dress was long and green, with a lace collar.

Síofra suspected her strange costume was in honour of the Green Man Festival.

"*What in the Lord's name have we here?*" Spellbinder hissed. Then she placed the mask on the table and placed her hands on her hips.

"Mrs Spellfinder, I would like you to meet my friend Síofra!" Cara proclaimed, in a voice that sounded more assured than she felt.

"The housemaids told me that you had brought someone with you. Is she a bird too?"

"No, I am not a bird. However, I am very pleased to meet you, Mrs Spellfinder," Síofra said as she stuffed a piece of toast and jam into her mouth. Then she let out a ginormous belch.

"Well, I never saw such terrible manners in a young girl. Not in all my years. Where did you come from?"

Síofra tried to speak – however, her mouth was so full that she was unable to.

"I rescued Síofra, Mrs Spellfinder. Her father is a fisherman who fell off his boat during a storm. I found her and I brought her back with me."

Mrs Spellfinder cast a beady eye on Síofra. Then she stepped closer to her. So close that Síofra noticed a curious thing. Around Mrs Spellfinder's neck hung a silver pendant. The pendant was shaped like a hare. It reminded Síofra of the witches in the witches' meadow.

Mrs Spellfinder prodded Síofra in the cheek with a pointy fingernail. "Well, she can't stay with us. Look at the state of her. She looks more like a boy than a girl and how on earth does she have a head of white hair? It's not natural."

"Please, Mrs Spellfinder, Síofra has nowhere else to

111

go to. Please let her come to Enniscorthy with us."

"What if someone comes looking for her, Cara?"

"We can tell one of our neighbours where she is. We can't just leave her here. Síofra could work as a chambermaid. You are always saying that you could do with an extra pair of hands."

"You really have it all figured out, don't you?"

"Perhaps the girls could help you with the preparations for the Green Man Festival," Kitty suggested.

Cara's eyes widened in disbelief. What was Kitty thinking?

"Alright, Cara, if your father agrees to it then Síofra can come to Enniscorthy with us. There is still a lot to be done before the festival takes place. We are making masks and hats. You two can help out with it. It will keep you out of mischief. Kitty, come to the kitchen. I need to speak to you."

"Yes, Mrs Spellfinder," Kitty replied and she winked at the girls as she left the room.

The girls burst out laughing as soon as the contrary old lady left the room.

"You don't have to help out with the Green Man Festival if you don't want to, Síofra. It is dreadful. All those people prancing around in masks and chanting. I don't like it one bit. And what if the Booley Girls or worse still what if the Green Man appears? He could unleash his anger on you."

"Cara, we must take part in the Green Man Festival, don't you see? If there is a chance that the Booley Girls and the Green Man will appear, then my mother could be there too. It might be my only chance to rescue her. We might even save Banshee Island."

"The thought of it scares me, Síofra."

"You need to be brave, Cara. I won't let anything happen to you, I promise," Síofra said reassuringly. However, it was a promise that she was not sure she could keep. The Green Man was truly terrifying. Her mother was the most powerful banshee that ever lived and even she was no match for him. How on earth could two young girls stand up to him? Síofra swallowed down her fear with the last of her breakfast. Her friend was right, there was something peculiar about Mr Crooks and Spellfinder. Síofra knew that she would have to keep an eye on them.

Síofra followed Cara out of the dining room and up the staircase. She stared at all of the paintings. They were of men, women and children. They were all dressed in the most elaborate dresses and suits. There were animals in the paintings too. Peacocks and dogs.

"Who are all of these people?"

"They are my ancestors."

"Do you know any of their names?"

"No, but this one is my favourite. I think that the woman is ever so pretty."

Cara pointed up at a painting of a woman in a long green gown.

Síofra gasped. She recognised the woman right away. The painting was of her mother. She must have sat for it on the same day that she married the Green Man.

"Wait, Cara! The woman in this painting is not your ancestor."

"How do you know, Síofra?"

"I know because the painting is of my mother."

"Of course! How have I not seen it before? She is beautiful. Just like you."

Síofra could feel the heat rise in her neck. She was not used to receiving compliments.

"Where is the painting of the Green Man and my mother on their wedding day?"

"It is there."

They moved a little way up the stairs and Cara pointed at a painting.

Síofra gasped at the sight of her beautiful mother sitting on a golden throne. She had the same eyes as Síofra. The same pale skin. Behind her, with his hand on her left shoulder, was a hideous man with a face like a goat and hooves for feet.

"I don't understand why these paintings are here in Soul Shadow Manor, Síofra. It seems strange to have a painting of him on his wedding day in our home."

"Apparently the Green Man was a friend of your family."

"You can't be serious, Síofra. Why on earth would my grandparents have been friends with such a wicked man?"

"The same reason why my mother married him. He must have cast some sort of spell on them."

"Your mother looks so kind, Síofra."

"I wish I could remember her, Cara. However, I was only a baby when I last saw her. Do you think she misses me?"

"I am sure that she does. We have only just met and even I can't bear to think of you going away again."

They moved on up the staircase.

"Where is your mother, Cara?" Síofra asked when they reached a landing.

Cara stopped. "I am not sure, Síofra. My mother was a shapeshifter. Part woman and part swan. However, she made a deal with a wicked witch."

"Why on earth would she do such a thing?"

"My mother fell in love with my father. However, a swan could never marry a man. So she asked the witch to take away her wings. However, the witch told her that on the day that her first daughter was born her wings would come back and she would have to fly back home to the land where she came from."

"I have heard this story before. It was written in *The Book* of *Dark and Scary Folktales from Long Ago*. However, I always thought it was a folktale, not a true story."

"I wish it was, Síofra, truly I do. The Green Man and the Swan Shapeshifters are all real. I wish that I had listened more carefully to the stories that Grammy used to tell me."

The smile fell from Síofra's lips. She had no way of knowing if she would ever see her mother again and, even if she did, she might not want to know her.

"Are you alright, Síofra? This house and all the people must be so much for you to take in."

"I am fine, Cara. I am tired, that is all."

"Come on. Grammy's room is this way."

Cara led Síofra along the landing.

"That is the room that once belonged to Aunt Róisín," she said.

Síofra longed to enter the bedroom. It might hold the answers as to what happened to her and the

Booley Girls all those years ago. She knew that the Booley Girls needed her help. Perhaps that is why she felt drawn to this house, to solve the mystery of Róisín's disappearance.

They stopped in front of a bedroom door.

Cara knocked on the door.

A small voice came from inside the room. At first, Síofra thought it belonged to a child. However, as the voice became louder, she recognised it as the voice of an elderly woman.

"It's me, Grammy – Cara. May I come in?"

"Cara, you came back! Come in, dear child!"

Cara pushed the door open and stepped into the room.

The room was painted white and filled with beautiful bouquets of vibrant violets. The window was open and a thin curtain billowed in the breeze. In the centre of the room was a four-poster bed. A woman was propped up on a pile of fluffy pillows. Her white hair was curled and fell about her shoulders. Her pale face was covered by a black veil. Two large blue eyes shone out from beneath the veil. The woman wore a black bed-jacket adorned with pearls. It was secured around her neck with a black ribbon. Long lace gloves covered her fingers. She held out a trembling hand.

"Come to me, my dear child, and let me see you."

Tears fell from the old lady's eyes.

She took out a handkerchief from up her sleeve and dabbed at her cheeks.

Cara knelt by her grandmother's bed. "It's alright, Grammy. I am safe. There is someone I would like you to meet."

Síofra walked up to the bed.

"Who is this?"

"This is Síofra. She is my friend," Cara announced proudly.

"Oh, Síofra, you are most welcome. I am Rose, Cara's grandmother. I am delighted to hear that Cara has a friend. Children need company."

She started to cry again and Síofra wondered if she was crying for Róisín. She felt sorry for the old lady and sat on the edge of her bed.

"Please don't cry, Rose. Róisín isn't far away from you."

"Whatever do you mean, child?" Rose lifted the black veil. Her paper-thin skin was lined like a map. Two large red patches appeared on her pale cheeks. Her eyes widened in disbelief.

Síofra leaned in close and whispered. "She is still here in this house. I have seen her with my own eyes.

Although I think that she is trapped somewhere in the Mists of Time."

"*No, Síofra! That is enough!*" Cara said angrily.

Her words stung Síofra like a nettle. She did not understand what she had done wrong. She was only trying to help.

"We have to go now, Grammy. Father has gone to prepare the carriages. Mrs Spellfinder will be in soon to dress you. I'll see you later."

Cara kissed her grandmother on the cheek, then she grabbed Siofra's arm and yanked it.

"*Ouch, that hurts!*"

"I'm sorry, Síofra, but we really have to go."

"Wait, come back!" the old woman cried. "What did you mean by saying that Róisín's spirit is trapped in the Mists of Time? Did you see her in Soul Shadow Manor? It can't be. It is not possible. Why won't she appear to me?"

Rose became hysterical, crying loudly.

Mrs Spellfinder bounded into the room with a face like thunder. She ran to Rose's side.

"Whatever is wrong, Your Ladyship?" Then she cast an angry look in Síofra and Cara's direction. "You two get out of this room immediately. I will not have you upsetting Her Ladyship like this. Cara, you will pay for this. You miserable wretch!"

Tears fell from Cara's eyes.

"I am sorry, Grammy," she said as she strode out of the room.

She ran along the hallway and back down the stairs. Síofra followed her. She could not understand what she had done wrong and why Rose was so upset at the mention of Róisín's name. Surely she would want to make contact with her daughter's spirit? It didn't make sense.

Suddenly Kitty appeared out of the dining room.

"There you both are. I thought I had lost you again. Here, put these on and get into the carriage. We are going to Enniscorthy right now." Kitty handed the girls two black cloaks with hoods.

"What about Grammy? We can't leave her here."

"Don't worry, your grandmother will follow us later." Kitty hurried the two girls out of the house and into the carriage that awaited them.

Chapter ten

THE BANSHEE AND THE SWAN

Sunlight streamed into the window of the horse-drawn carriage. Four white horses were bridled and waited patiently for the driver to lead the way. The two girls sat opposite each other. Cara had her arms folded across her chest. Tears stained her cheeks. The feathers in her wing were ruffled.

Síofra did not know what she had done to make her friend so angry. "What is wrong, Cara?"

"Nothing."

"Tell me."

"Why did you tell my grandmother that you could see Róisín?"

"Because I thought it would help her."

"Help her? How could you possibly know what would help my grandmother? You had only just met her."

"Your grandmother is sad. She misses Róisín terribly. Her heart is broken."

"That is none of your business, Síofra."

Cara's words stung like a bee-sting.

"Silver was right. I should never have come here. I thought that you were my friend and that you cared for me. However, all you have done is order me about and I am sick of it. I want to go home."

Cara gasped. "No, Síofra. You don't mean it."

"Yes, I do. I would rather be surrounded by the souls of the dead than live in the Land of the Living." Síofra's heart thumped in her chest. Yet she did not feel the urge to cry. Silver's words of warning were ringing in her ears. *"You must not go near the girl, Síofra. No matter how much you want to. I forbid it."* Guilt bloomed like a rose in Síofra's chest as she thought of her poor aunt.

"I gave up everything to be here with you, Cara. Perhaps the other children are right not to play with such a spoiled girl as you. Spellfinder was right. You are a miserable wretch."

Tears fell from Cara's eyes.

"Stop the carriage! I want to go home," Síofra demanded.

"No, Síofra. It's not safe. I can't leave you alone at the side of the road! Anything could happen to you."

"That is a chance I am willing to take. Tell the driver to stop or I will jump out of the carriage while it is moving."

"Please forgive me, Síofra. I didn't mean to upset you."

"It is too late for that now."

Síofra pounded on the roof of the carriage with her fist.

"You don't understand, Síofra. You have to be careful in the Land of the Living. Not everyone will accept you as I do. If anyone finds out that you are a young banshee they will punish you for it."

Síofra understood all too well. She knew that she should have stayed away from people in the Land of the Living, just as Silver had told her.

Suddenly the carriage ground to a halt.

"Is everything alright in there, miss?" James the driver shouted.

"My friend would like to get out of the carriage, James."

The girls waited for the carriage to stop.

123

"Before I go, Cara, there is something that you should know."

"What is it?"

"Róisín has been sitting next to you this entire time."

"What do you mean? Róisín is a spirit, not a person. You said so yourself."

"Yes, she is, and I intend to find out exactly what happened to her. Ghosts only haunt the living when they are unhappy."

Síofra looked into the ghost girl's eyes. She wore a long red skirt and a blue shawl about her shoulders. Above her right eyebrow was a small cut. It appeared to be bleeding. She bore a striking resemblance to Cara. Yet the spirit of Róisín seemed to be lost. She could not see Síofra or Cara.

Tears sprang from Cara's eyes. "My Aunt Róisín disappeared thirty years ago. It can't be her."

"Not all ghosts go to the afterlife straight away. Not if they have unfinished business in the Land of the Living."

"Unfinished business. Whatever does that mean?"

"I don't know. However, I suspect that she is unhappy."

"Can you speak to her, Síofra, and ask her what is troubling her?"

"No, not unless she speaks to me and she hasn't

said a word yet. Róisín appears to be trapped in the Mists of Time. She can't find her way out. She may be still alive. Her desire to come home may be so strong that she is appearing as a ghost."

James opened the carriage door.

"It is not safe for you to get out," said James, "and we need to move on. There are Redcoats everywhere. They are hiding in the woods, waiting to pounce."

"I will not stay where I am not wanted."

"Please don't leave me with a ghost," Cara whispered into Síofra's ear.

"You do not need to worry, Cara. Spirits can't harm you. It is the living you must fear."

Síofra repeated the words that her Aunt Silver had spoken to her many times on Banshee Island. Although she did not believe that Róisín was truly dead. It felt more like she was lost and could not find her way back home.

She turned and walked away.

She regretted leaving Banshee Island. She should never have trusted Cara. However, she was there for a reason. The Curse of the Booley Girls had to be broken and Síofra knew that she was the only one who could do it.

Part Two

Come away, O human child!

To the waters and the wild

With a faery, hand in hand,

For the world's more full of weeping

than you can understand.

'The Stolen Child' – W.B. Yeats – 1886

Chapter eleven

THE WITCHES' TRAP

Silver stormed out of The Spectacular Library of Magical Things and down the two hundred stone steps. She was furious with herself for telling Síofra the truth about her parents. The young banshee should have returned home hours ago. Could it be possible that she disobeyed her orders and left Banshee Island? It did not bear thinking about. There had been many stories over the years. Stories of how people in the Land of the Living had treated banshees and witches. The horrors of witch trials and drownings were still fresh in her mind. Silver could not cope if anything happened to Síofra. She had already lost her sister – to lose Síofra too would completely break her heart.

"*Síofra!*" Silver screamed out into the air.

The sky cracked open like an egg. Thunder and lightning streaked across the sky. The waves crashed against the rocks. Silver ran through the Forest of Lost Souls and on towards the graveyard. When she reached it she ran over to the stone angel and bowed her head.

Then she uttered some words in the hope that the ghost girl Róisín would hear her. "Please help Síofra. Don't let anything bad happen to her. She is all I have."

Silver fell to her knees. Sadbh flew down from the branch of a tree and landed on her shoulder. Silver reached out her hand and stroked the owl's soft feathers.

"At least I have you, Sadbh, my old friend."

Suddenly a sound came from the Forest of Lost Souls. Silver jumped to her feet. She was not expecting the arrival of any souls on the Island. Her heart leapt with joy. "*Síofra!*" she cried.

The thunder and lightning stopped and the sun rose in the sky. Silver ran as fast as she could into the forest. Of course Síofra didn't leave her. She would never do such a thing. How could she even have thought it? Birds sang in the sky. Sunlight glistened through the trees. Silver followed the sound that led her straight into the meadow, where a coven of shapeshifting witches waited for her.

Chapter twelve

SHAPESHIFTING HARES

The witches formed a circle around Silver. They banged loudly on their bodhráns and danced a peculiar dance.

Suddenly one of the large black hares broke free from the circle. She stepped closer to Silver. The hare stood tall on her long hind legs. Her wet nose twitched beneath brown eyes. Silver tried to run but there was no escape. She was bewitched and could not move from the spot. It felt as though her feet had grown roots that were buried deep in the ground.

"Let me go! Please, I am begging you!" Silver cried.

The hare that was the head witch opened her mouth to reveal yellow teeth.

"The promise has been broken, Silver. Up until this day witches and banshees have lived side by side, since we were banished from the Land of the Living. We agreed that we would never allow a human to set foot on Banshee Island."

Silver screeched as she struggled to get free. Her long white hair flowed over her shoulders.

"I don't know what you're talking about. I have not broken the promise. Let me go!"

The witches hissed and cackled.

"You brought a stranger to this island. You and your niece will regret it."

"If you have done anything to harm Síofra you will pay for it."

"Don't worry, your precious niece is safe for now. However, she was in such a hurry to leave you that she left this behind."

The witch bent down and picked up the blue piece of sea glass from the long yellow grass. Silver recognised it straight away.

"Síofra's sea glass! Give it back to me!"

"Not until you tell us how that girl got on the island."

"What girl? You are not making any sense."

"Perhaps this will jog your memory."

An old haggard witch with a lump on her nose

appeared from behind a rock. Her back was twisted. She held a cane in her left hand and in her right hand held a small black case. She opened the case and took out a monocle.

"Look through this and all will be revealed."

Silver placed the monocle up to her right eye. She squinted her left eye and a vision appeared before her of Síofra and Cara sailing in Mamó's boat towards the Land of the Living.

Silver pulled off the monocle and threw it into the fire. The flames turned blue.

"What kind of magic is this? Síofra would never leave this island and I don't know who that girl is. I have never seen her before."

Silver knew that the witches were capable of anything and could not be trusted.

"So you don't believe us? Well, where is your precious niece? You don't have the faintest idea where she is, do you?"

As much as Silver hated to admit it, deep inside her heart she knew that what the witches were saying was true. Síofra had gone to the Land of the Living. However, that still didn't explain about the girl.

"Please let me go. I believe you but I need to find Síofra. She is in great danger in the Land of the Living."

Silver was terrified that Síofra would go looking for her mother. The young banshee was no match for the wickedness of the Green Man.

"It is not just your niece who is in danger. If that girl tells a living soul about what she saw on this island it could be the end of all of us."

"No, you are mistaken. Even if the girl does tell anyone about what she saw, they would never believe her. Besides, the island wouldn't let a living soul onto its shores."

"You are a fool. If the girl got here, then others will follow. It is only a matter of time. The island isn't as strong as it used to be."

Silver knew exactly what the witch meant. Banshee Island used to be a powerful place. It was full of magical creatures such as birds who flew backwards and fish who could survive on land. There used to be many different types of plants there too. Such as sunflowers that the witches used in potions to cast weather spells and buttercups that produced real butter, and the catmint flower that purred whenever the sun shone. However, in recent years all of these magical creatures and plants had simply vanished and even the more normal animals and plants were disappearing gradually. The island was getting weaker.

The witch pointed her long green fingernail in Silver's face. "There is only one thing for it. We need to cast a spell to make the island invisible for another seven years."

"No! You can't do that! Síofra won't be able to return. Please give Síofra a chance to come home. She will be back soon, I am sure of it. Let me go and find her. Then together we can work out a way to protect Banshee Island and to ensure that people from the Land of the Living can't reach us."

The witches cackled.

"You are not going anywhere. If you leave this island we will not let you back again."

"Please! I need to find Síofra."

"If your niece cared about you and Banshee Island, she would never have left in the first place. Síofra has until the sunsets in two days' time. After that we will cast the invisibility spell. If Síofra is not back here by then it will be too late. She will be banished forever."

Then the witch threw Síofra's sea glass. It spun through the air. Silver reached out her hand and caught it.

Then she tried to move her feet but when she did she fell to the ground. She stood up and ran as fast as she could out of the witches' meadow. Her heart thumped in her chest. What was Síofra thinking of? Such a reckless act would cost them all dearly. It wasn't just their own lives at stake. The souls that arrived at the island depended on the banshees to welcome them. If they weren't there then they might never reach the afterlife. There was no way of knowing if Síofra would make it back to the island in time. Silver knew that if she didn't, then she would be destined to stay in the Land of the Living forever more and there was nothing that anyone could do about it.

Chapter thirteen

LOST IN TIME

As night cloaked the shoulders of daytime, Síofra was scared. Never in all her life had she felt so alone. How foolish she had been to trust Cara! She was walking back in the direction that the carriage had travelled, hoping to find her way to Soul Shadow Manor. Once there she would find a way of crossing the sea to Banshee Island. However, she had entered an ominous forest and was utterly lost. The moon shone down on her and owls hooted in the trees. Trees waved their spindly branches at her. Síofra realised that she would have to find somewhere to stay for the night until she figured out a way of getting back home.

It was then that she spotted a hawthorn tree. It

reminded her of the tree back home. Síofra lay beneath the tree. Then she used her cloak as a blanket, curled up like a cat and drifted off to sleep.

She woke with a start. Had she heard voices? She looked all around her and there was no one to be seen.

"Who is there? Show yourself!" she cried.

Suddenly the sound of laughter and music reached her ears.

"People," Síofra said to herself.

She walked in the direction of the singing. It sounded like girls' voices. Following the sound like a fox following a scent, she arrived at the foot of a mountain. She longed to be back on the island tucked up in bed, listening to Mamó's stories about the little people and how they lived in the palms of giants. Fear tightened its grip on her heart.

She turned around to go back. However, a thick green fog swirled like soup around her ankles and she couldn't see the ground in front of her. She shuddered, remembering mention of a green fog in the Green Man story in the *Dark and Scary Tales from Long Ago*.

Then, again she heard the sound of girls' voices singing as sweetly as bluebirds on a summer's day.

We are seven
seven are we

friends forever
forever we will be
alone on the mountain
singing our song,
green mist descended
everything went wrong,
so come up and find us
if you dare
The Booley Girls of Wexford
will meet you there.

"The Curse of the Booley Girls! Be brave, Síofra," she said to herself. If only Silver was here she would know what to do. However, Silver wasn't there.

She began to climb, following the sound of the singing. It grew louder and louder as she climbed.

The thick green fog became heavier. She couldn't see where she was going. She kept climbing. At last she knew she must be close to the singers. She hurried forward and, stumbling, fell forward onto the ground, crying out as she did so. She had fallen on grass and was not hurt. She got to her feet.

It was then that she saw them: six girls, each wearing a long red dress. Blue shawls were tied in knots around their shoulders. Each of the girls held a candle and stood in a circle in front of a small hut made of stones.

They were looking in Síofra's direction.

"Did you hear that?" a young girl with long red hair cried.

"What? You are imagining things, Maeve!" a second girl with a head of blonde curls replied.

"No, I am not, Mary. I heard someone crying out."

A taller girl broke the circle and walked towards Síofra. The thick green fog was up to her waist. She held her candle high.

"I heard it too. I think that there is a ghost in the mist."

The Booley Girls! Síofra could not believe her eyes. Six girls on the mountainside, singing their song. However, there should have been seven. One was missing. They heard her but somehow thought that she was a ghost.

Síofra suddenly realised that she had travelled back in time. As far as the Booley Girls were concerned, she was the ghost. Could they even see her?

"Don't be scared! I have not come to harm you!" she cried as another girl with a yellow headscarf charged forward. She was holding a pitchfork and she waved it in the air, narrowly avoiding Síofra.

"I want to go home, Bláthnaid!" the small girl called Maeve cried.

"Stop crying like a baby, Maeve," said the tall girl.

"We can't go home even if we want to. The mist is too heavy. We must wait until morning. And we need to find Róisín – she's been missing for three days now."

"What if the ghosts have got her or, worse still, The Green Man?" said Maeve. "Oh! I can hear the rattle of his Death Coach – I am sure of it."

Síofra knelt behind a rock and watched as six petrified girls huddled together.

Maeve covered her ears with her hands and screamed. The terrifying sound cut through the air like a knife.

"For goodness sake! Mary and Deirdre, get her inside," said Bláthnaid. "These ghosts just come to torment us. I'm sure they love to hear Maeve scream!"

Mary and Deirdre led Maeve into the hut.

"I can't hear any rattle now," a short girl with a pink bow in her hair said.

"We haven't seen the Green Man in three days, Sarah. Perhaps he has forgotten about us."

Síofra could not believe her ears. The girls were being tormented by ghosts every night and they were scared that the Green Man would come for them. Worst of all, Róisín had left the group. She was all alone, lost in the Mists of Time.

Before she knew what she was doing, Síofra bounded out from behind the rock.

"Don't be scared!" she said. "I won't harm you."

The girls' eyes darted here and there. Clearly they couldn't see her. She picked up a small bird's skull and hurled it towards the girls. They stared at it in amazement. Sarah and Bláthnaid screamed and ran into each other's arms.

Síofra cried, "Please trust me! I have come to help you!"

Maeve ran back out of the stone hut. Deirdre was with her. They wielded pitchforks and waved them around wildly.

"Who are you? Show yourself!" Maeve ordered.

"I am a friend from the future. Can't you see me?"

"It's a trick!" Bláthnaid cried.

"Leave us alone. There is nothing here for you. We are god-fearing girls," Maeve said.

If only they could see me, Síofra thought. Then they would know that I will not harm them.

Then the distant rumbling of carriage wheels and the rattling of chains alerted the girls to danger. They all screamed.

"Quickly! Back into the house!"

"What about the cows and the butter we churned?" Bláthnaid cried.

"Leave them where they are. We can fetch them in the morning."

"If we survive the night," Maeve said as she covered her head with her shawl and ran for cover.

Síofra ran back through the mist and hid behind a boulder. She could hardly believe her eyes. A large black carriage, driven by four black horses with feathers on their heads, hurtled towards her through the fog. It was then that she saw a terrifying sight. The Green Man, with his triangular-shaped face and hoofed feet, was sitting on the roof of the carriage.

Síofra noticed the face of a woman peering out of the carriage window. A black veil covered her face. *My mother*, Síofra said to herself, although she had no way of knowing if the woman in the carriage was her mother or not. She rubbed her eyes with the back of her hand. She felt as though she must be dreaming. The carriage did not stop at the hut. It hurtled on up the mountainside.

As soon as the coast was clear, Síofra ran as fast as she could through the thick green mist. Her mind was racing as fast as her heart. How had she stepped back in time? And how would she find her way back again?

Síofra just put one foot in front of the other and ran down the mountainside.

Then the sound of carriage wheels echoed in the darkness behind her. The Green Man had turned the carriage around and was chasing her through the fog.

I must not look back, she said to herself.

She reached the forest and plunged into it. After a while she couldn't hear the sound of the Death Coach anymore but she kept running.

She didn't see the tree stump until it was too late. She screamed as she fell onto the forest floor and hit her head off a rock.

Chapter fourteen

ENNISCORTHY

"There she is!" Cara cried.

Séamus O'Leary ran over to Síofra. Her head was bleeding.

"She must have fallen over this branch and hit her head on a rock. What were you thinking of, leaving her alone, Cara? I am disappointed in you."

"I tried to stop her, Father, I told you – but she insisted on getting out of the carriage."

Séamus carefully picked Síofra up. Then he placed her in the carriage and dabbed her forehead with a kerchief. "It's a nasty cut."

Tears fell from Cara's eyes as she placed a blanket over Síofra.

"I will ride on ahead," said her father. "Look after her, and if she wakes up do not let her out of the carriage, do you understand me?"

"Yes, Father," Cara said as her father shut the carriage door.

"I am so sorry, Síofra. I should never have let you go," Cara whispered into her friend's ear. She held her wing close to Síofra's body.

* * *

Síofra woke as the carriage trundled into the ancient town of Enniscorthy.

"Where am I?" she cried.

"Síofra, you are awake!"

"Cara, you came back for me! There is something I must tell you." Síofra winced. There was a throbbing pain in her head. "*Ouch*, my head hurts!"

"Hush, Síofra, you have had a bad fall. All that can wait."

Síofra peered out of the carriage window. She had never seen such a delightful place. The whimsical town was full of winding streets and tall, enchanting buildings. A crystal-blue river meandered through the centre of the town. There was a magnificent castle, with turrets reaching up into the clouds. The entire town appeared to have been built on a hill. People were coming and going along the bustling streets. Boats drifted along the river. Síofra could hear the sound of people singing on a boat as it passed beneath the old bridge.

"Where are all those people going to?" she asked.

"They are making their way up to Vinegar Hill to set up camp and to prepare for the battle."

Suddenly a pudding-shape hill erupted in the distance. There was a mill on top of it. Crowds of people were gathering there. Síofra's heart sank like a stone. She knew that battles brought death and this made her sad. She turned to look at Cara who had a worried look on her face.

"Where is your house, Cara?"

"I live not far from here in Daphney Castle."

"It sounds wonderful." A small smile flickered across Síofra's lips.

"Yes, I suppose it is. It is close to the River Urrin and has a moat. The best thing of all is that there is a tunnel beneath the castle that runs directly under the town!"

"I am so glad that you came back for me, Cara."

Síofra moved closer to Cara. She placed her head on her shoulder. Cara covered her with her wing.

Thoughts of the Booley Girls and the Green Man drifted like feathers through Síofra's mind. What had happened last night? Had she really seen the Booley Girls? Did the Green Man chase her? Could the woman in the carriage have been her mother? There were so many questions that she did not have the answer to. Perhaps she had imagined it all. Suddenly the coach ground to a halt.

James opened the door of the house.

"Nice to meet you again," he said as he helped the girls out of the carriage.

The castle was much smaller than the one they had just passed in the town. They walked over a small bridge. Síofra peered into the moat where a pair of swans glided gracefully over the water. Suddenly she felt homesick. She thought of the golden swans back on Banshee Island, carrying the souls of the dead to the afterlife. She longed to see the evergreen trees in the Forest of Lost Souls. I wonder if Niamh is still there? How I miss my little fox! Then she felt a pang of guilt. How will Silver manage without me, she thought. What would have happened if the Green Man caught me last night? I must be more careful.

Cara and Síofra stepped off the rickety bridge. Then they walked through the ivy-clad gates. There was a large oak tree at the entrance of the castle. Síofra placed her hand on it. She recalled the Tree of Memories on Banshee Island and wondered how many souls had arrived since she left.

"Stop dawdling and get inside right away. You promised me that you would help with the Green Man Festival. It is only a day away, you foolish girls!"

Síofra turned to see Mrs Spellfinder standing in front of the wooden castle door. She wore a long green dress and mask shaped like a sheep's head. She tapped her foot impatiently. Síofra had hoped that they had left Mrs Spellfinder behind them in Soul Shadow Manor. All this talk of the Green Man Festival was making her feel dizzy. She needed to tell Cara about the vision that she had of the Booley Girls.

"Come on," Cara whispered, then she held Síofra's hand as they stepped into Daphney Castle.

It took a moment for Síofra's eyes to adjust to the darkness. The walls were covered in wood panelling and the family's coat of arms hung over a large fireplace. There were stuffed birds in glass cabinets. Their beady eyes stared at Síofra. Stags' heads hung from the wall. Síofra shivered. It was cold and damp. She wondered how anyone could live in such a dark and dismal place.

"Father likes to hunt. He caught all of these birds while travelling overseas. Then he had them shipped back here."

Síofra did not like to think of all the birds being hunted. She hoped that their spirits lived on somewhere else.

Mrs Spellfinder lit the candles in the candelabra that hung from the low ceiling. The sunlight struggled to enter the narrow windows.

It was then that Síofra noticed something. Above the door, there was a stone gargoyle, with its mouth open. She had to cover her mouth to stifle a scream. The gargoyle looked like the Green Man. Why would Cara's family have such a hideous thing in their castle? Síofra guessed it was for protection. People seemed to believe that they had to please the Green Man or else he would harm them. What a terrible way to live!

Mrs Spellfinder stepped in front of Síofra and Cara. Then she wagged her finger at them. Her large eyes bulged. The veins in her neck were visible beneath her paper-thin skin.

"You two girls have got some explaining to do. Don't think you have got away with disappearing like that, Cara O'Leary. There is something fishy going on here and I will get to the bottom of it. Mark my words."

The sound of a piano playing stopped Mrs Spellfinder in her tracks.

"Father's home. He came ahead of us on his horse." Cara grabbed Síofra's arm and pressed on a panel in the wall which turned out to be a hidden door that led into a library full of books.

"Cara and Síofra, you have arrived! How are you feeling now, Síofra? You got a nasty bump on your head." Séamus stopped playing the piano and twirled his moustache between his finger and thumb. He was dressed in a pair of brown trousers and a long grey overcoat.

Síofra placed her hand on her head. It still hurt but the bleeding had stopped. "I am quite well, thank you. I do appreciate your coming back for me."

"Cara insisted on it. Although I do not know why you decided to leave the safety of the carriage in the first place."

"Forgive me, sir."

"Take care next time or the banshee might get you."

"If only he knew," Cara whispered to Síofra.

Then she ran like paint onto a canvas into her father's open arms.

"You look sad, Father, what is wrong?" Cara placed her hand gently against her father's cheek.

"The battle I told you about will take place soon. I need you to take care of your grandmother – can you do that for me?"

"Why can't I go with you, Father? You promised me I could."

"It isn't safe up there, Cara."

"I want to go. When we were coming into town I saw children my own age going up onto Vinegar Hill, to camp and prepare for battle."

"The people don't realise that they are in great danger. Besides, you are not like the other children. Your wing makes you special." He traced one of Cara's feathers with his finger.

"If it is so bad, Father, then why are you going?" Tears fell from Cara's eyes and onto the piano keys.

"I don't have a choice. People are depending on me."

Cara understood. Her father was one of the leaders and he had to be there to defend the town.

"Oh, Father, I love you," she said, then she placed her wing around him.

"Enough of the tears, Cara – you need to be a big strong girl for me – can you do that?"

"Yes, Father." Cara hated lying to her father, but she didn't have a choice.

"Why don't you take Síofra out on a tour of the place. You'd like that, wouldn't you, Síofra? I heard some of the older people have arranged a festival for the Green Man up on Mount Leinster. Why don't you get Mrs Spellfinder to take you there? I am sure that it would be a bit of fun and you would be away from the fighting. Mrs Spellfinder has been making those wretched masks for weeks now."

"I didn't think that you would agree with the festival, Father?"

"Why ever not?"

"Well, I have discovered that your twin sister Róisín was a Booley Girl and she disappeared thirty years ago. Many people think that the Green Man had something to do with their disappearance and that the girls will appear again tomorrow night."

"Nonsense, Cara! I can't believe that you of all people would listen to that."

"What was Róisín like, Father?"

"She looked like you, Cara, and she had a gift for healing people. I remember when we were small children, people would call to see her when they were sick. Róisín could cure them."

"You must miss her, Father."

"All that was a long time ago, Cara. Besides your

poor grandmother does enough grieving for the both of us. Do you two girls have a costume for tomorrow night?"

"No, Father. Mrs Spellfinder said that we have to help her to make masks later in Doyle's Barn."

"Won't that be fun?" Séamus stared into his daughter's eyes. She was so serious all of the time.

"I suppose so, Father," Cara replied, then she glanced over in Síofra's direction.

Thoughts of the Green Man festival had turned Síofra as pale as a ghost. She couldn't wait to get Cara on her own. Then she could tell her that she saw a vision of the Booley Girls.

Suddenly the living-room door swung open and a young boy ran in. Mrs Spellfinder chased after him with a sweeping brush.

"I tried to stop him, sir, but he insisted on seeing you."

"That's quite alright, Mrs Spellfinder."

Cara recognised the boy straight away. His name was Finneas Pepper. His father was a carriage-maker. He had a mop of blonde hair and large blue eyes. He sat behind her in school and pulled her hair. Kitty told Cara that boys did that sometimes when they liked girls. Cara thought that it was a funny way of showing it.

Finneas was out of breath from running.

"Sir!" he panted. "I have a message for you."

"Yes, Finneas, what is it?"

"You have to go to Vinegar Hill right away, sir. English Soldiers are getting closer. They have been spotted marching from Ferns."

"This is not good. Mrs Spellfinder, tell James to saddle up my horse."

"Right away, sir."

"Cara, go to the kitchen and ask Kitty for a drink for Finneas and a bite to eat."

"Yes, Father."

"Remember what I told you, Cara. You must not go to Vinegar Hill under any circumstances. Do you understand me?"

Cara did not answer. Instead she ran into her father's open arms once more.

"Please be careful, Father."

"I will do my best, Cara," he promised.

Then he walked over to the corner of the room and picked up a musket.

Moments later he was gone.

Chapter Fifteen

FINNEAS PEPPER

"There you go, Finneas Pepper! As soon as you drink your milk and eat your biscuits you can leave."

"Charming as ever, Cara," Finneas replied. Then he turned to look at Síofra who was leaning against the piano. "Who is this boy?"

Cara blushed. "This is not a boy. This is my friend Síofra."

"Why is she wearing boys' clothes? And why is her hair white? Did she get a fright?"

Cara stamped her foot. It was one thing for Finneas to insult her but she would not allow him to insult her friend. "You are a rude and insolent boy!"

Síofra giggled into her cupped hand. She thought it

was hilarious the way that Cara was sticking up for her.

"It's alright, Cara," she said. "I can stand up for myself."

Síofra held out her right hand to Finneas. He took it and shook it.

"You certainly shake hands like a boy."

Síofra laughed out loud and Cara turned her eyes up to the ceiling.

Seconds later Kitty came into the room.

"Finneas, do you have any news about the battle?"

"Hello, Kitty. Yes. I have some bad news. The Redcoats are advancing more quickly than we thought. It looks like the battle on Vinegar Hill will have to take place first thing tomorrow."

"Oh no, my family are camped on Vinegar Hill! My Aunt Alice and my cousin Andrew."

"I am going back up there now. Do you want me to get a message to them?"

"Yes, that would be great."

Cara gulped. "You are not going to fight in the battle, are you, Finneas?"

"My mam says every man, woman and child must play their part. I have my own pike and everything."

Cara sat on the piano stool and twirled a strand of

her hair between her finger and thumb. "Not everyone is fighting. Father said that I have to stay here. He wants me to go to that dreadful Green Man Festival on Mount Leinster tomorrow night."

Síofra placed her hand on Cara's shoulder.

Finneas frowned. "And rightly so. The battle is no place for children. I would give anything to be going to the Green Man Festival."

"Why don't you join us, Finneas?" Cara said, smiling.

"I can't, Cara. It wouldn't feel right to go to a festival when I am needed to fight for my country."

Kitty pulled a kerchief out of the pocket of her apron. It was embroidered with the initials K. D.

"Give this to my Aunt Alice, will you, Finneas?"

"It would be my great pleasure, Kitty."

Finneas walked over to the door, then he turned to face Síofra and Cara.

"Pleased to meet you, Síofra. Any friend of Cara's is a friend of mine."

Cara's neck turned as red as a tomato. She picked up the last of the biscuits from the plate and handed them to Finneas.

"Here, take these. You will need your strength for fighting those Redcoats – and don't get yourself killed, Finneas Pepper."

A huge smile erupted on Finneas's face.

"That is the nicest thing you have ever said to me, Cara O'Leary."

Kitty started to bawl her eyes out.

"Goodbye," Finneas said, then he ran out of the castle and on toward the battle with a spring in his step and hope in his heart.

Chapter sixteen

NO ESCAPE

Silver sat on the edge of the cliff. She studied the piece of sea glass that she held in her hand. The golden sun radiated orange rays, which made the sea appear green.

"Oh Síofra, why did you have to leave me?" Her heart ached. It didn't bear thinking about what would happen if Síofra found her cry on the Land of the Living. People there hated banshees. They would hunt Síofra down like a fox if they knew her real identity.

Silver took a deep breath. The island would turn invisible when the sun set in two days' time. She had to put her own feelings aside and do what was best for everyone.

She tied her hair up with a green-velvet ribbon and pulled her black cloak over her head. Then she ran down to the seashore. The small green boat that had washed up on the shore was still there. Silver had wondered who it belonged to. Now it was clear to her. It was the boat that the girl arrived on. It had been battered in the storm, but there were no visible holes and Silver knew that she had to take the chance. She hoisted the sail.

Sadbh flew onto her shoulder. "Hello, my old friend." She stroked the owl's soft, downy feathers. Sadbh swivelled her head as the boat was sailing away. Silver turned back to look at her home one last time. Golden swans flew through the air. Her house jutted out from the cliff face. Niamh, Siofra's fox cub, stood on the shore.

Sadbh flew onto the sail.

Then with a determined look in her eye Silver took the rudder and steered the boat towards the Land of the Living. She hoped with all her heart that she would find Síofra and bring her home before it was too late. However, as she started to steer the boat away from the island, she was washed back onto the shore.

Silver screamed at the top of her lungs. She realised that the witches had used their magic to put an invisible shield around the island so that she couldn't leave. All Silver could do now was sit on the shore and hope that Síofra came home before Banshee Island disappeared forever.

Chapter seventeen

GIRLS IN HORSE-HEAD MASKS

Cara ran to the window and Síofra followed her. They watched Finneas go until he became no more than a tiny speck in the distance.

"I hope that he survives, Síofra. He can be annoying sometimes, but all boys are, aren't they?"

"I don't know. I have never met a living boy before."

"Count yourself lucky," Cara said, sniggering.

Suddenly there was a loud bang on the library door. Síofra and Cara turned around and were shocked to see three young girls standing there. Each of them was wearing a straw mask shaped like a horse's head. The frightening masks covered their faces and their necks. In their hands they held straw dolls.

"Who are you and how did you get in here?"

"We are the Booley Girls, the Booley Girls are we! Give us some pennies and we will leave you be!"

Cara screamed. Síofra walked over and pulled the mask off one of the girls' heads.

"Sarah Murphy, is that you?" Cara cried.

The young girl giggled.

"Yes."

"I will not give you any money. Get out of here right away. I'll tell your ma and da that you are going around scaring people. That is a rotten thing to do."

Footsteps outside the room and the rattling of keys told them that someone was on their way. Spellfinder bounded into the room with her hands on her hips.

"What on earth is all this commotion about? Did I hear you scream, Cara?"

"Yes, Mrs Spellfinder. I got a fright when these three came in and said that they were the Booley Girls. Get them out of here right away. It's not right, making fun of the Booley Girls. Here, take your ugly mask and go!"

Spellfinder threw her head back and laughed raucously. "You are foolish, Cara. I have always wondered what goes on in that head of yours. These are three young girls from town. They are trying out their costumes for tomorrow night's festival, aren't you, girls?"

"Yes, Mrs Spellfinder!" the girls chimed.

"There is no harm in it. Just a bit of fun. Run along now, girls. I will meet you in Doyle's Barn at noon. We will be practising our dances and choosing who will lead the procession."

The girls ran giggling from the room.

"What procession?" Cara enquired.

"The procession up the mountainside. You two girls must come too. You can help us to make the straw man. You will need costumes too. There is so much to be done." Mrs Spellfinder waved her hands in the air.

"I don't want to take part in the Green Man Festival," Síofra announced.

"You don't have any choice. You will do as I tell you. Insolent girl!"

"You shouldn't be messing with things that you don't understand."

"Síofra is right," Cara agreed. "It is thirty years ago today that the Booley Girls vanished and who knows what might happen?"

"Shut up, the both of you! The Green Man Festival has taken place every mid-summer for centuries."

"What about the rebellion? You should call it off."

"We will do no such thing. It will be a welcome distraction for the older people and the children. You will both be at Doyle's Barn at noon and that is an order."

Mrs Spellfinder stormed out of the library, banging the door behind her.

Chapter eighteen

THE GIANT MAN MADE OF STRAW

"The Green Man Festival can't go ahead, Cara."

"I agree with you, Síofra, but how can we stop it?" Cara ruffled her feathers as she spoke.

"We will think of something."

"We should go to Doyle's Barn and see what Spellfinder has planned. Maybe it's not as bad as we think."

"Alright, Cara. I could do with some fresh air."

Síofra and Cara walked out of the dark castle. The sunlight stung their eyes. Síofra noticed an old rope swing that hung off the oak tree.

"Can I have a go, Cara?"

"Of course. As long as your head doesn't hurt too much."

Síofra jumped onto the rope. She gripped it with both hands and laughed as the swing flew over the moat.

Síofra jumped off the swing when it was mid-flight and landed with a thump on a mound of grass.

Cara held out her hand and helped her up.

"Why don't you have a go, Cara?"

"No, I only have one hand."

"That shouldn't stop you. Your wing will help you to fly."

"It's not just my wing."

"What is it then?"

"I wish I could wear trousers like you, Síofra. Dresses are a nuisance when riding horses or swinging on rope swings."

"Why don't you get a pair of trousers made?"

"Father would never allow it."

"Why not? Your father seems like a kind man. Surely he would let you wear what you want"

"I already get made fun of because I have a wing instead of an arm. Dressing like a boy would make things even worse."

"That is a shame. Silver lets me wear whatever I want."

"She sounds amazing."

"Yes, Cara, she is. You remind me of her." Síofra smiled as she thought of Silver.

"Really? You must miss her."

"With all my heart."

They walked along the narrow road that led up the mountain to Doyle's Barn. It had low stone walls on either side.

"Síofra, I feel dreadful about everything that happened between us. I am sorry for all the horrible things that I said to you. When I saw you lying on the side of the road with that cut on your head I felt awful. How can you ever forgive me?"

"You must not blame yourself, Cara. It was my choice to come here to be with you."

"Maybe one day we can return to Banshee Island together."

"I would like that, Cara. The poor island!" She shook her head. "It isn't as magical as it used to be."

"Do you really think that the animals and plants on the island are going extinct due to the Curse of the Booley Girls?"

"Yes, I do, Cara." Síofra's stomach lurched as she thought of what happened during the night. Did she really step back in time and visit the Booley Girls? Or was it all just a dream?

"What is wrong, Síofra? You look so worried."

"Cara, there is something very important that I must tell you."

"Did something terrible happen to you last night?"

"Yes, it did."

"I knew it."

Cara reached over and linked Síofra's arm as they crossed a small bridge over a stream.

"I still can't make sense of it all."

"Tell me. Maybe I can help."

"I fell asleep beneath a beautiful hawthorn tree and was woken in the middle of the night by the sound of voices singing. I got up and followed the sound. Suddenly a terrible fog appeared. It swirled around my ankles and within moments I could not see the ground before me."

"You must have been terrified."

"Yes, I was, Cara. All I kept thinking was that if anything happened to me then poor Silver would be left on her own. I came to the foot of a mountain. I heard the singing again and followed the sound up the mountain."

"I am confused, Síofra – there are no mountains near the place you left the carriage."

"That's what I thought. But suddenly the fog lifted

and I spotted six girls standing in a circle holding candles. They turned to look in my direction. I shouted out to them. But the strangest thing happened."

"What was it?"

"The girls could hear me but they couldn't see me."

"Perhaps it was the fog."

"I thought so at first. However, they mentioned ghosts visiting them at night-time."

Cara gasped. "You mean they thought you were a ghost?"

"Exactly."

"Did you see my Aunt Róisín?"

"No, Cara. Although I heard the Booley Girls discussing her. They said that Róisín had been missing for three days."

"How awful!"

"She must have wandered off on her own and got lost in the Mists of Time."

"Poor Róisín! She has been all alone for thirty years. We need to find a way to help her, Síofra. There must be a reason why you can see her."

"I agree, Cara. I truly believe that Róisín needs my help."

"What happened next?"

"The girls heard the sound of the Death Coach and

hid inside the stone hut. Next thing, the Death Coach came trundling up the mountainside."

"Was the Green Man there?"

"Yes, and a woman was sitting inside the carriage. She wore a black veil over her face. Like she was in mourning."

"Could it have been your mother?"

"Possibly. I couldn't say. I ran off down the mountain and then I heard the carriage behind me. As I entered the forest, I tripped and fell – and blacked out. The next thing I remember is your father calling my name."

Cara suddenly stopped. "Do you hear that? It's music."

"What is that?" Síofra said, pointing.

She could not believe her eyes. There, a little way off the road, was a straw man. He was extremely tall, propped up on wooden stilts and dressed in mismatched green clothing.

"It looks like a giant scarecrow!" Cara cried then she ran over to a stone wall where she could get a closer look. "It must be the straw man that Spellfinder mentioned. It is supposed to represent the Green Man."

A group of men sat on the ground nearby. They were wearing straw masks and banging on drums. The three girls from earlier had been joined by four

171

more and they were dancing around a maypole. A group of boys wearing antlers on their heads were playing strange music on cow horns.

"Is that Doyle's Barn?" Síofra asked, pointing to a large wooden structure.

"Yes."

They climbed over the wall and made their way to the barn. Reaching it, they walked around its corner to find the entrance and were confronted by a great big hobby horse. The horse's head was an actual horse's skull and its body was covered in a white sheet.

"*There you are!*" it snarled.

The voice was Mr Crooks'.

Suddenly Spellfinder stepped out of the barn.

"Oh, so you found them, Mr Crooks!" she said.

Cara gulped. She did not know that the wicked Mr Crooks was there. He was angry with her for stealing his boat. She longed to go back, but then Spellfinger gripped her wing.

"What kept you so long, girls?"

"We stopped to play on the rope swing," Cara explained.

"I might have guessed." Then she let go of Cara's wing and a bunch of feathers drifted onto the grass. "*Into the barn, everyone!*" she yelled.

People appeared from behind trees and bushes. They all wore costumes made of straw.

"All these people should be fighting in the rebellion. Dressed in those costumes they would frighten the Redcoats away!" Cara whispered to Síofra who nodded in agreement.

Inside the barn the costumes that people wore were even more elaborate. One man wore a wolfskin over his head. His face peered out from inside the wolf's jaws. There were men dressed up as women and women dressed as men. The musicians played a peculiar song and people danced around broomsticks. Síofra had never seen such an odd gathering before. Flowers hung from the rafters.

Spellfinder jumped up onto a makeshift stage. "If I could have your full attention, please!"

The crowd fell silent.

"Now, as you all know, we have celebrated the Green Man Festival for hundreds of years. Our ancestors wore costumes just as we do now and they performed the Green Man Hunt around the mountainside. This year many of our family members – our sons, daughters and grandchildren – will be fighting for our freedom against the redcoats. We stand in solidarity with them by continuing with our ancient festival."

People stamped their feet and clapped their hands in approval.

"Now, as you know, every year we ask the youngest girls to choose a person to be this year's Green Man. Sarah Murphy, would you step forward, please!"

"Oh no. It's one of those horrible little girls who called to the castle this morning. I bet she picks me." Cara sighed.

"Now, to make things fair, young Sarah will close her eyes. Then I will spin her around three times. Then she will walk into the crowd with her eyes closed and the first person that she picks – man, woman or child – will be this year's honorary Green Man!"

Sarah shut her eyes tight. People started to chant *"The Green Man is coming! The Green Man is coming!"*

Spellfinder spun the young girl around three times. Sarah stretched her arms out in front of her and walked toward the crowd while a man dressed as a clown followed her every move and made people laugh.

"She's coming this way, Cara," Síofra said to Cara then she tried to walk away but people pushed her back.

Seconds later she felt a small hand grip her wrist.

"We have this year's Green Man!" Spellfinder announced.

"No, Cara, help me!" Síofra screamed.

Cara tried to reach Síofra but the swell of the crowd was like the waves in the ocean. Two men dressed as women lifted Síofra high above their heads. Then they carried her to the stage.

"*Put me down!*" Síofra cried.

"As you wish!" said one of the men and they dropped her at Spellfinder's feet like a sack of potatoes.

"*Well, well, well, if it isn't Síofra, our new arrival!*" Spellfinder hissed.

Mr Crooks pranced about the stage in his hobby-horse costume and the sea of faces laughed at him.

Síofra pulled herself to her feet.

"There has been a mistake. I am not supposed to be here. I don't want to take part in the festival. Please let me go."

"Let you go? Why, you have only just got here!"

Suddenly insults were fired at Síofra like coins in a fountain.

"*Is it a boy or a girl?*" a man behind a bear mask shouted.

"*Great costume!*" a girl with a hen beneath her arm chipped in.

"*How dare you! This is not a costume! These are my real clothes!*" Síofra shouted back.

"*What's wrong with her hair?*" one snotty-nosed boy with an axe in his gloved hand shouted.

"Let her go!" Cara pushed her way to the front of the crowd.

People instinctively backed away, not wanting to get too close to the girl with a wing.

"Careful! Mama said if you touch her wing you will burn!" a girl said to her friend as Cara passed.

"I said let her go!" Cara walked up onto the stage.

Her shawl fell from her shoulder and the crowd gasped. Many had never seen her so close before.

"That girl has a wing!" a boy with a crooked chin and broken teeth shouted.

"Hush now, everyone!" Mr Crooks shouted from beneath his horse-head. *"This is Cara O'Leary. Her father is one of the leaders of the rebellion!"*

"What do you mean by showing me up like this?" Spellfinder hissed. Her eyes bulged.

Cara saw her own reflection in the glassy pupils.

"Síofra said that she doesn't want to be the Green Man."

"She has no choice in the matter!" a man with a mask that looked like a pig's head yelled.

Cara looked at the angry crowd. If she could see their faces, they might not be so brave then.

Spellfinder sounded the cow's horn and there was silence. *"Let them go! I know where to find them.*

Síofra, you will be our Green Man whether you like it or not."

"Quick, Síofra! This way!"

Cara gripped Síofra's hand and together they ran through the angry sea of animal faces. When there were outside they gasped for air. The shadow from the huge Green Man scarecrow hung over them.

"Let's get out of here, Síofra, before they change their minds."

As quick as a flash, Síofra and Cara climbed over the small wall and ran along the road. Fields full of golden corn spread at each side of the road.

"What was all that about?"

"They want you to be their Green Man, Síofra."

"I gathered that but what exactly does it mean?"

"It means that you will dress in green and wear a hideous mask. Then you will be told to run as fast as you can and hide. After a short while, the people attending the festival will chase after you. The person who captures you will be crowned Queen Green or King Green and they will parade you around in a carriage for all to see."

"That sounds terrifying."

"It is and there is always a chance that you will get hurt. I heard a story of a boy who was chosen to be the

Green Man many years ago. The angry crowd chased him into a river and he drowned. Another girl fell off the mountain and died. Let's go into town, Síofra. They wouldn't dream of following us there. Not today anyway, with the battle about to commence. They wouldn't want anyone to see them in their silly costumes."

"We can't, Cara. You father forbade it."

"Father said that I can't go to Vinegar Hill. He didn't say anything about not going to town."

Síofra smiled. "I suppose you're right."

Suddenly the sound of voices and horse-hooves alerted the girls. They swung around and saw two grubby-faced children hurtling towards them on a horse and cart. They were heading in the direction of town.

"Oh no! I didn't think today could get any worse!" Cara cried.

"What's wrong?"

"The children on that horse and cart are from my school. The ones that I told you about."

"The children that are bullying you for having feathers?"

"Yes." A melancholy look cast a shadow on Cara's face.

"Just keep walking, Cara. We have as much right to be on this road as they have."

The cart pulled up beside them.

"Well, well, well, what have we here? It is only Her Ladyship out for a walk. Would you not think of flying like your cousins the swans?" the boy said, sniggering.

He had bright red hair and freckles. He was sitting on a sack of potatoes and chewed on a piece of straw as he spoke. He appeared to be about fourteen years old. A younger girl sat on his right-hand side. The girl wore pigtails on her hair and had a gap between her front teeth. She scratched her head and Cara guessed that she had nits. The children giggled and pointed their dirty fingers at Síofra.

"Well, Miss Fancy Pants, aren't you going to introduce us to your new friend?"

"Go away, Charlie Byrne!"

"Too important to speak to the likes of me, are you?"

"Yes, she is!" Síofra shouted. Then she stamped her foot and grabbed Cara's arm.

"Oh, it speaks!" Charlie sniggered.

The girl sitting beside Charlie was holding a small white kitten on her lap.

"Look, Charlie, her hair is as white as my kitten's

179

fur. She's as weird as the Bird Girl. They suit each other."

The children erupted with laughter.

Síofra's cheeks burned with anger. She noticed that the children had pikes on the back of the cart and a large picnic basket overflowing with food. They were heading for the battle on Vinegar Hill.

"Where are you going to anyway, Cara?" the boy asked.

"It's none of your business, Charlie Byrne."

"I bet you're not going to the battle on Vinegar Hill, like everyone else. Your daddy wouldn't allow his precious girl to get her wing dirty!"

He and the girl burst out laughing again.

"Ignore them, Cara," Síofra whispered into Cara's hair.

"As a matter of fact, Charlie Byrne, that is exactly where we're going. We're going to fight on Vinegar Hill with the rest of the town."

"No, Cara!" Síofra warned.

"I bet those Redcoats will be quaking in their boots when they see you running towards them with a pike in one hand and a wing flapping in the breeze. What kind of a bird are you anyway? A pigeon or a goose?"

"Leave her alone!" Síofra hissed.

"Birds are supposed to have two wings. Or else they can't fly. You are a rubbish girl and an even worse bird!" Charlie sniggered.

"I will show you, Charlie Byrne." Cara said. "Just you wait and see!"

"Where are my manners, Miss Fancy Pants? May we offer you both a lift on our humble cart?"

"No, you may not. We would rather walk, thank you!" Síofra exclaimed.

"You two are lousy liars!" the girl said. "There's no way that you're going to Vinegar Hill!"

"Yes, we are, and I will prove it to you. We will accept your lift, Charlie Byrne."

A look of horror crossed Síofra's face. "No, Cara. You must not get onto that cart. The battle will be too dangerous. It is not safe. You promised your father that you wouldn't."

"I am going, Síofra, whether you come with me or not. It will be one way to stop Spellfinder from making you take part in that silly Green Man Festival."

Charlie held out his grubby hand and helped Cara onto the cart. The girl moved over to make room.

"Well, are you coming or not? We haven't got all day, you know!" Charlie said.

Síofra did not want to go to the battle. However, she

could not leave Cara, not now, and she didn't much like the prospect of dressing up as the Green Man and being chased across the fields. The one question on her mind was what happened when they caught the Green Man? The thought of it terrified her.

"Yes, I am coming and I am perfectly capable of climbing onto your cart without your help."

"Suit yourself," Charlie said.

Síofra was barely on the cart when Charlie shook the rains. "*Charge!*" he shouted at his old horse, Bess.

Cara fell back as the horse ran towards the ancient town as fast as her legs could carry her.

Chapter nineteen

THE BATTLE OF VINEGAR HILL
21st June 1798

The sun shone down on Vinegar Hill. The children followed the procession of people making their way through Enniscorthy Town. The ancient streets were bustling with activity. It felt like a fair day rather than the day of a great battle. Horses grazed on Pig Market Hill and the River Slaney flowed beneath the old bridge. Charlie had to steady the old mare as they trundled down Castle Hill. Síofra looked into people's faces. They had a determined look in their eyes. They would not be beaten.

"Look, Síofra!" Cara said as she pointed up to Vinegar Hill. The smell of smoke filled the air. "The rebels have set the heather on fire. Father told me that they would do that to call all the people to fight."

"Well, it seems to be working," said Siofra as people gathered all around them.

Charlie drove the horse and cart up to Vinegar Hill. People from the town and surrounding countryside had set up camp on the hill. There were thousands of men, women and children. It was a truly spectacular sight to behold. On top of the hill was a windmill.

"I have never seen so many people before," Síofra said as she climbed off the cart.

Charlie helped Cara down. "Well, I guess this is where we say goodbye, Cara."

Síofra noticed that there were tears in Charlie's eyes. The thought of the impending battle frightened him too. His sister ran on ahead towards a plump lady in a blue dress.

Cara had never seen Charlie look so sad before, and she almost felt sorry for him as he unloaded the pikes from his cart.

"Thank you for the lift, Charlie."

"You are welcome and I am sorry for all the times that I made fun of you in school."

Cara's eyes opened wide in disbelief. She had never seen Charlie like this before. He obviously wanted to make peace with her, in case he did not survive the battle.

"I accept your apology, Charlie. You had better go – your ma is looking for you."

Charlie nodded and ran into the small brown tent to be with his mother.

As day turned to evening, music and laughter filled the air. People sat around campfires. They held their hands out to the flames. A woman with a headful of dark curls sang a battle song and the sky turned pink overhead. An old woman with a face lined like a map offered the girls a bowl of mutton stew, which they ate hungrily. Then as the stars lit up the sky, the sound of music and laughter died away. People knew that it would not be long before the battle commenced.

Síofra and Cara sat against a tree. They huddled together to keep warm. It had been a hot day, but the evening brought with it a cool breeze. Cara draped her wing around Síofra's shoulder.

"It is a beautiful night, Síofra," Cara said as they watched a star shoot across the sky.

"Yes, it is the summer solstice. The shortest night of the year."

Síofra could not help but think of Banshee Island. There was always a great celebration on the summer solstice. The souls of the dead would gather by the seashore and tell each other stories about their old lives. Silver would cook a great feast and they would sing songs. Something about the way people had gathered on Vinegar Hill reminded her of it. She guessed that many of them would make their way to Banshee Island before the night was over.

"Cara, what are you thinking of? You look so wistful."

"I was thinking of my mother. How I wish I could be a shapeshifter like she was. But I am neither human nor shapeshifter. I was born with one wing, but it is useless as I can't fly."

"You are perfect the way you are, Cara."

"You may think so, but I saw the way the townsfolk look at me. They think I am cursed. I know it. Spellfinder hates me."

"Spellfinder seems to hate everyone."

"Yes, but she detests me because of my wing and I don't blame her. I am a freak of nature."

"You shouldn't be ashamed of who you are, Cara. However, I know exactly what that feels like. I know that I am destined to become a banshee. Yet I know that people on the Land of the Living hate me. They blame the banshee for taking away their loved ones."

"People fear what they don't understand, Síofra."

"Your father seems very nice."

A small smile flickered across Cara's lips. "I feel so

grateful to him. He has always been there for me."

"I understand. I feel the same way about Silver. She gave up everything to raise me."

"Perhaps that is why we get on so well together, Síofra. We both know what it is like to be different."

"I felt drawn to you from the first time I saw you, Cara. Like a moth to a flame. It felt as though we were destined to be together. You must think that I am silly." Síofra felt heat rise in her cheeks. Perhaps she had said too much. She peered at Cara, who had tears in her large green eyes.

"Oh, Síofra, I don't think you are silly at all. I felt it too. Deep within my heart. I dreamt that one day we would meet. Kitty thought I was strange for wanting to meet a banshee. Yet I knew that we had to be together. We are both different to everyone else."

Síofra squeezed Cara's hand and smiled.

"Cara, is that really you?"

"Finneas!" Cara jumped up and threw her arm around Finneas's neck. "We are having a wonderful time. I did not believe that a battle could be so much fun."

Finneas pulled away from Cara. He bit his bottom lip. "The battle has not started yet. You have to go home before your father finds you here."

"Where is Father? Have you seen him?"

"I saw him earlier. He is in a tent in the centre of a field, deciding on the best strategy to adopt to defeat the Redcoats."

"Poor father. He has a lot on his mind."

"He has and he does not need another thing to worry about. You both must leave here right away. Go back to Daphney Castle. Lock the doors and stay there until it is safe to come out. I mean it, Cara. There is no place for you here."

Cara was hurt by Finneas's words. "You don't think that I am as good as other girls because of my deformity. Síofra is the only one who ever truly accepted me. She understands what it is like to be different." Tears stung her eyes as she spoke.

Finneas's eyes widened in disbelief. "No, Cara, you are wrong. Your wing is not a deformity. It makes you more beautiful and special than any other girl in the whole world. You are unique."

Cara's jaw dropped in disbelief.

"It is because I care about you so much that I want to make sure that you are safe," said Finneas.

"We can't go home, Finneas. Spellfinder insists that we must take part in the Green Man Festival."

"That silly old festival isn't still happening, is it?"

"It is."

"After everything that happened with the disappearance of the Booley Girls, you'd think that they would have learned their lesson."

The sound of gunfire alerted them to danger. The battle of Vinegar Hill had begun.

Finneas joined a line of men who ran forward towards the oncoming soldiers. The air filled with smoke. Women and children screamed and a crowd of people ran for cover.

Suddenly the girls were separated. Cara was terrified.

"Síofra, where are you?"

"I am here, Cara. Take my hand."

Cara reached out through the darkness. Her fingertips touched Síofra's. Then she screamed and her hand fell to her side as a stray bullet hit her in the chest and she fell to the ground.

"*Cara!*" Síofra screamed.

Then she ran like a lightning bolt over to Cara and held her in her arms.

She laid her down gently on the ground, as all around them soldiers fought. Blood stained Cara's feathers.

Cara looked up at Síofra, at her white hair glistening under the moonlight. She'd loved Síofra

189

with all her heart. She was her best friend. No one had ever understood her the way that she did.

"Is the battle over yet, Síofra?"

"No, Cara, it has just begun," Síofra replied.

Then she was overcome with the urge to cry as she realised that Cara would have to battle for her life. How could it be that they had just found each other and now this had happened? It was the saddest thing that had ever happened to Síofra. Hot, angry tears sprang from her eyes like flames from a fire. She rocked Cara back and forth then she wailed to the sky.

Síofra had finally become a real banshee.

The crowd of people who had gathered around the two girls covered their ears at the sound of the shrill cry.

"It's the cry of a banshee!" a woman with bright-red hair cried.

People gasped in amazement.

"God save us!" an injured soldier wailed. Then he blessed himself.

"Don't leave me, Cara!" Síofra cried.

Cara closed her eyes.

"*No,*" Síofra screamed.

Suddenly Finneas appeared in the crowd.

"*Let me through!*" he bellowed. There was blood on his shirt.

He picked Cara up in his arms and carried her away from of the battle. Her wing hung limply by her side.

Síofra ran after him, wailing.

"She's a banshee!" a man shouted. *"Look at her white hair! We will not win the battle tonight with her here. Get her away!"*

"Finneas!" Síofra screamed. *"Where are you taking her?"*

"I will take her to the makeshift hospital on Court Street!" he said.

"Banshee!"

Síofra swung around to find a hostile crowd with pikes facing her. She suddenly recalled Silver's words and realised that she herself was in grave danger.

"I have to go, Finneas! Promise me that you will take care of Cara for me!" Her voice was barely audible over the sound of the angry mob that was moving toward her. Guns fired in the distance. She could hear the shouts and screams of soldiers as one by one they fell on the ancient hill.

They will write songs about this one day, Síofra said to herself.

"Get her before it is too late!" screamed the woman who had given the girls bowls of stew.

191

Silver is right, the living can never be trusted, thought Síofra. Her heart broke as she kissed Cara on the forehead and fled from the crowd.

The soldiers were surrounding the hill from all sides. They were firing their muskets at the men who were only armed with pikes. Síofra used the cover of gun-smoke to make her escape. She saw a white horse with a brown patch around its eye. It was tied with a rope to a tree. She undid the rope and wiped the tears from her eyes with the back of her hand. Then she climbed on the horse's back and made her way down the side of Vinegar Hill and on towards the deserted town.

Chapter twenty

THE BANSHEE'S GREAT ESCAPE

The entire town of Enniscorthy had become a battleground. Men in red coats charged towards Vinegar Hill. They fired guns and canons. The heather was blazing. It was a terrifying sight.

Síofra stared up at Vinegar Hill. Flames danced in the air. She could see people running through plumes of smoke. Tears streamed from her eyes as she thought of Cara. She hoped and prayed that Finneas would get her to the hospital before it was too late.

No one noticed her as she arrived on horseback at the gates of Daphney Castle. The soldiers were all focused on the battle on the hill.

She jumped off the old white mare and tied her to a

tree. "Thank you, girl." She patted the horse on the back.

Then she saw Kitty. She was standing at the door.

"Síofra, what is heaven's name has happened to you? And where is Cara?"

"Kitty, I need your help. But it is not safe to speak here."

"Come to my chamber quickly."

Kitty gripped a candle in a golden pewter candlestick from a table. Then she took Síofra's hand and led her up some stone stairs into a small, damp attic room.

"Sit down, girl. Have a sip of water." Kitty helped Síofra over to a chair and handed her a cup of water. She noticed a bloodstain on her cloak.

Síofra was trembling with cold and shock. She turned to Kitty.

"Cara is hurt, Kitty."

Kitty placed a hand over her lips.

"Oh no! Where is she?"

"Finneas took her to the hospital on Court Street."

"We must go to her! How did she get hurt? She was forbidden from going up Vinegar Hill."

"I know but Spellfinder wanted to make me the Green Man in this year's festival. We needed to get away so we took a lift on a cart with some boy called Charlie Byrne."

"That little rascal! Wait till I get my hands on him! He is nothing but trouble, that boy."

"You mustn't blame Charlie. It was my fault. I should have protected Cara."

A ferocious sound erupted outside the castle as an angry mob banged against the door.

"Whatever is that commotion all about?"

"The people have come for me, Kitty."

"For you? I don't understand."

Síofra jumped to her feet. She felt like a deer caught in a trap. Then she gripped Kitty's hands and stared into her eyes.

"Can I trust you, Kitty? Please say that I can."

"Of course you can trust me. Whatever is the matter?"

Síofra knew that she was taking a risk telling Kitty the truth about her identity. Yet Cara had told her that Kitty was trustworthy and she needed her help.

"I am not an ordinary girl, Kitty. I am a banshee. The people on the hill heard me cry when Cara got shot. I didn't mean to cry, Kitty, honestly I didn't. If Cara dies I will never forgive myself. Please, Kitty, help me! I am scared that I am going to cry again and if that happens I could kill you too."

Kitty looked at Síofra. Her heart went out to her. The poor young girl really believed she was a banshee. Perhaps it was because she was born with a white head of hair. Or maybe it was the blow to the head she received when she fell in the forest.

Suddenly there was a loud knock on Kitty's door. Síofra screamed.

"Hide beneath my bed, Síofra, quickly!"

Kitty ran to the door and opened it.

Finneas stood there with tears in his eyes.

"Finneas, come in quickly."

"Cara has been shot, Kitty."

"I heard, Finneas. I can't believe it." Tears streamed from Kitty's eyes.

"The surgeon in the hospital said that she is going to be alright."

"Thank God!"

"All she kept saying to me was to help Síofra. But I can't find her anywhere and there is an angry group of people outside being led by Mr Crooks of all people."

Síofra crawled out from under Kitty's bed.

"There you are, Síofra." Finneas smiled through the tears.

"Did I hear you right? Did you say that Cara is going to be alright?"

"Yes, she is. But you won't be unless I take you to safety."

"Take me to Soul Shadow Manor, Finneas."

"Why on earth do you want to go there?"

Síofra didn't know whether or not she could trust Finneas yet. Cara told her that he could be mean sometimes. If she told him that she was a banshee and needed to get back to Banshee Island then he might hand her over to the angry mob. All she needed was for Finneas to take her safely to Soul Shadow Manor – then she could get a boat across to the island and home to Silver.

"I want to go there because it will be far enough away from town. No one will think of looking for me there and my real home is close to the Manor."

"Alright, Síofra, if that's what you want. But we will need your help, Kitty, to distract the people."

"Of course, Finneas."

Kitty placed her arms around Síofra and gave her a big hug.

"You take care of yourself, Síofra, and you are welcome back here anytime. Any friend of Cara's is a friend of mine."

"Thank you, Kitty."

The sound of footsteps outside Kitty's chamber alerted them to danger.

"Kitty, come here right away. I am looking for that wicked girl."

"Oh no! It's Mrs Spellfinder. I have to go. I will get rid of her. When the coast is clear go as fast as you can."

"Kitty, get here this instant!" Spellfinder's voice boomed.

Kitty jumped. "I have to go." Then she ran out of the bedroom.

Chapter twenty-one

THE BANSHEE'S CRY

"The coast is clear!" Finneas whispered as he beckoned Síofra down the stone steps and outside the castle.

Síofra shuddered. Tonight she had found her cry. Now she was a true banshee. It felt as though something inside her had changed forever. Síofra watched as Finneas ran over to the stable and saddled a horse.

"Quick, Síofra. We have to go before Spellfinder and that angry mob return."

Síofra ran over to Finneas who had mounted the horse. He stretched his hand down and helped her up.

"Hold on to me, Síofra – we will have to move fast."

Síofra pulled her hood up and placed her arms

around Finneas's waist. This must be what it feels like to have friends, she realised. Her mind was spinning. There was so much to take in.

"Finneas, listen to me. What the people are saying about me–"

"That you are a banshee. I know that's rubbish. People around here are superstitious – they believe in things like banshees. My mam told me that years ago a poor woman was driven out of Wexford by an angry mob who said she was a banshee. Don't worry, Síofra, I am not going to let anything like that happen to you, I promise."

Síofra gasped. Finneas was referring to Silver. Oh, how Síofra's heart ached for her! Since finding her cry Síofra's emotions felt heightened. The magic contained within a banshee's heart was so strong. Síofra feared it and she feared herself. At least now she knew that she could trust Finneas with her secret.

They made their way through the village of Bree and on towards Wexford. Síofra realised that she would have to find a way for Finneas to believe that she was a banshee. He needed to know that he was placing himself in danger just by being with her.

"Can we stop for a moment, Finneas?"

"Stop? Here in Oylgate? Whatever for? We have a

long journey ahead of us and the Redcoats could jump out and capture us. It's a chance we can't take."

"Please, Finneas. It won't take long."

"If you insist. But we are only stopping for a few minutes. Do you hear me?"

Finneas jumped off the horse and tied it to a tree.

"I will never understand girls. Not for as long as I live," he muttered. Then he made his way over to Síofra.

She was sitting beneath a tree. The flickering embers of a small campfire glowed in the darkness. It was left by soldiers who had gone to the battle of Vinegar Hill.

Síofra was sitting on the dew-stained grass with a large toad on her knee.

"Where did you get that ugly toad from?" Finneas asked.

"Hush, Finneas," Síofra said. Then she stroked the toad's slimy back and shut her eyes. Moments later she started to cry and wail. She rocked back and forth, all the time holding the toad in her hands. Tears fell from her eyes, like raindrops from storm clouds.

Finneas looked on in amazement as she dropped the toad onto the grass. Then he realised that the toad was stone dead.

He turned and strode back to the horse.

Síofra followed him.

"Now do you believe that I am a banshee, Finneas Pepper?"

"No, I don't believe it. For all I know that toad could have been about to die before we came along."

Síofra grabbed Finneas by the wrist and stared into his blue eyes. Freckles danced like starlight across his nose. He was a kind-hearted boy. She needed him to know the truth of who she was.

"I *am* a banshee, Finneas. Whether you believe me or not it doesn't change things. I have the power over life and death. If I cry for someone I can kill them."

"Then you can kill me?" A terrified look appeared in his eyes. His lip trembled.

"Yes, Finneas, I could. If I cry for you, then you could die. However, I cried for Cara and you said that she is still alive. I don't think that my cry is strong enough to kill a person yet. But I need you to know that if you join me then you are risking everything."

Finneas thought about what Síofra was saying. He could not deny what he just saw with his own eyes. He knew that he should turn his horse around and leave her to find her own way to Soul Shadow Manor. Yet something was stopping him.

"I can't leave you here, Síofra. I made a promise to

Cara that I would take care of you and I never break my promises."

The sound of English voices alerted them to danger. Two Redcoats were walking out of a tavern. Their golden buttons shone under the moonlight. They walked across the road to where the children stood.

One of the officers twirled his pointy moustache between his finger and his thumb. "What are you two doing walking the roads at this hour of the night?"

Finneas stepped forward. "We are on our way to visit our sick grandmother in Wexford town."

"Strange time of the night to go visiting, isn't it?"

Finneas bowed his head. "We heard the Banshee's cry which means that our granny could die before the night is out. Did you not hear it, sir?"

Síofra's eyes widened in disbelief. The soldiers turned pale.

"We did hear a strange wailing noise. I thought it was a cat."

"If you don't mind me telling you, sir, I think you should return to the tavern. The Banshee is walking these roads tonight and she is not one to mess with."

Síofra stifled a laugh. The soldiers were clearly spooked.

"You Irish and your strange superstitions! Be on

your way and give your grandmother our regards," the soldier with the moustache said.

Then they hurried back into the tavern.

Síofra and Finneas burst out laughing.

"That was hilarious. Did you see their faces?" Síofra had to hold her sides, she was laughing so hard.

"I only told them the truth about banshees. Little did they know that they had come face to face with one."

Síofra placed her hand on Finneas's arm.

"So you believe me? Thank you, Finneas."

"Now can we please get going before you cause any more trouble tonight?"

Finneas mounted and helped Síofra back onto the horse and, under the watchful gaze of the moon, they galloped towards Soul Shadow Manor.

Chapter twenty-two

THE VANISHING ISLAND

Soul Shadow Manor burst through the fog like a shooting star. Síofra looked over at Banshee Island. Something was wrong. The island was barely visible. It looked as though it was disappearing before her very eyes. She fell to her knees on the grass and Finneas bent down beside her.

"What is wrong, Síofra? You look as though you have seen a ghost."

"I have. Or at least I have seen the ghost of my home. Banshee Island is vanishing. I have to get back before it's too late."

"Here, let me help you. I will see if I can find a boat somewhere along the shore."

Tears fell from Síofra's eyes. All her life she had wanted to cry and to feel sadness the way that everyone else did. However, now that she could it was almost too much to bear. If she left the Land of the Living now, she would never see Cara and Finneas again. However, Banshee Island looked as though it was about to disappear. If that happened she might never get back. Síofra was a real banshee now, she had found her cry and with that came great responsibility. Responsibility to guide the souls of the dead to the afterlife.

She waited in great anxiety until Finneas returned at last.

"I can't find a boat anywhere, Síofra. Why don't you stay in the house tonight and in the morning you can find a boat to take you home."

"Alright, Finneas. It has been a long night and I could do with some rest."

"Things will be better in the morning. They always are."

"But how can we get into the house?"

"Don't worry – I know where the spare key is. Mr O'Leary gets me to do odd jobs for him in the summertime. He showed me where the key is kept."

"What a stroke of luck!"

Síofra followed Finneas through the walled garden.

Roses bloomed all around them. Even in the darkness the faint smell of roses filled the air. At the back of the walled garden was an old gate that led to the family's burial plot.

Síofra could not believe her eyes. There in front of her was a stone angel and it was identical to the stone angel on Banshee Island.

"Here it is!" Finneas lifted a small plant pot. Beneath it was a key with a green ribbon. A worm wriggled over it.

"Quickly, let's get inside in case Spellfinder or anyone from Enniscorthy comes looking for me," Síofra said.

"They would never know that you are here, Síofra."

"That may be true, Finneas, but I don't want to take any chances."

Síofra followed Finneas around the back of the crumbling manor house. He opened the door to the servant's entrance and Síofra followed him inside.

"Wait there a minute and I will light a lamp," he said.

Finneas lit an oil lamp on the kitchen table. Síofra pulled up a chair and sat down.

"It's freezing in here, Finneas."

"Yes, it is. This place gives me the creeps."

Síofra reached into her bag and took out *Dark and Scary Folktales from Long Ago*. Then she moved closer to the lamplight. Finneas took the book from Síofra and scowled.

"*Dark and Scary Folktales from Long Ago*. Why on earth would you want to read such a frightening book?

"Because it contains the story of the Green Man and the Booley Girls."

"The Green Man from the festival?"

"Yes, my grandmother used to read it to me when I was younger."

"Why would she read you a story about the Green Man?"

"To warn me to stay clear of him. You see ..." Síofra realised that there was no easy way to say it. "The Green Man is my father."

Finneas burst out laughing. "That is hilarious, Síofra. Don't you know that there is no such thing as the Green Man?"

"It's no joke, Finneas. I wish with all my heart that it was."

Finneas's eyes opened wide in disbelief. Either Síofra was losing her marbles or she was telling the truth. It was hard to know what to believe.

Síofra opened the book. The tale of the Green Man

was the fourth folk tale. There was a strange illustration of a man with a triangular face with a goat's beard and hooves for feet.

"He is a scary-looking thing. I'll give you that," said Finneas.

Síofra began to read. "*Once when the world was still young, when birds flew under the sea and fish swam in the sky, an old belief passed around from one generation to the next. No one knew where the belief came from – some say it travelled through the Mists of Time. The belief was that all the crops would fail unless they picked a person to be chased in a hunt down the mountainside. The people would gather at the turfcutter's cottage and then the chase would begin. As you can expect, no one wanted to be hunted like a fox. However, if you were chosen, there was no escape. One year a boy named Jack Green was picked. He lived with his father at the top of Mount Leinster. 'Please, Father, tell them I won't do it!' Jack cried. "You must do it, son, or else you will unleash an ancient curse on the land. Jack realised that he did not have any choice in the matter and the following evening the hunt began. The villagers gave Jack a head start. He ran across ditches and jumped over rocks until he discovered a goat standing alone on the mountainside. Jack stopped for a moment and looked into the goat's bright green eyes. Then out of nowhere a green fog descended on the mountain. Not a soul could see where they were going. Many people fell to their deaths while looking for young Jack Green. The next morning the death bell tolled for all those whose lives were lost on the mountainside. There were seven in total. They discovered young Jack Green the next morning sleeping in a field with a herd of mountain goats. However, people were shocked at his appearance. They hardly recognised it was him. His feet were hooves and he had a beard. His pupils were rectangular and two horns protruded from his triangular-shaped skull. The people ran to fetch the priest. However when they returned Jack Green had vanished. However, legend says that once a year on the day following the summer solstice the Green Man can be found driving the Death Coach and looking for the souls of those who have lost their way in life."*

Finneas shuddered. He could feel a chill in his bones.

"You say that this monster is your father, Síofra?"

"Yes, Finneas. He married my mother. There is a painting of her in the entrance hall here. The woman in the green dress."

"I have seen that painting!" Suddenly Finneas believed what she was telling him. "Your mother was beautiful."

"Yes, she was."

"Was your mother a banshee too?"

"Yes. I suppose that is why the Green Man wanted her. He knew that she could gather the souls of the dead."

"How did you escape?"

"My grandmother saved me. She brought me to Banshee Island." Síofra stifled a yawn. "I am fierce tired now."

"Go to bed and get some sleep."

"What about you, Finneas?"

"The sun is starting to rise, Síofra. I am going to travel back to Enniscorthy. It is a long journey. My mam and sister need to know that I am still alive."

"Will you check on Cara for me, Finneas? Give her this." She pulled Cara's golden swan ring off her finger. "Tell her that I miss her and I hope to see her again someday."

"I will, Síofra."

Síofra stood up and walked Finneas to the door. The early morning sun shone across the land.

"Thank you, Finneas."

"You are welcome, Síofra."

"Please don't tell anyone about me."

"I would never do that, Síofra."

Síofra stood in the doorway and watched Finneas

climb onto his horse. Hope bloomed like a flower in her heart. Finneas said that Cara was going to be alright. She might not have found her mother, but finding friends like Finneas and Cara was worth just as much. Síofra realised that she was ready to go home to Banshee Island now to cry for the souls of the dead.

Chapter twenty-three

AFTER THE BATTLE

The air was thick with smoke as Finneas made his way through Enniscorthy. The sun shone down on Vinegar Hill where only hours before the battle took place.

"Finneas!"

Kathleen, Finneas's eight-year-old sister, ran towards him. She was wearing a straw hat and had a green shawl tied around her shoulders. A straw mask covered her face. Brown gloves hid her hands. Tufts of straw stuck out of her black boots.

Finneas dismounted and knelt down in front of Kathleen. He loved his little sister. She was a kind and gentle girl.

Ever since their father died, Finneas had done his

best to care for his mother and sister. Guilt swam through his veins. He should never have left without telling his mother where he was going.

"Kathleen, is that you?"

"Yes, Finneas. I am dressed up for the festival tonight. It's going to be great fun."

"I don't want you going anywhere near that stupid festival, Kathleen, do you hear me?"

Kathleen placed her hands on Finneas's cheeks.

"Don't be upset, Finneas. Mammy said that we should be proud to come from Enniscorthy. We didn't win the battle on Vinegar Hill but we did our best and showed the Redcoats that we are brave."

"Mammy is right, Kathleen."

Finneas held his sister's hand and, leading the horse, walked up the island road to their house.

Finneas's mother May could not believe her eyes when she saw her son standing in her kitchen. She burst into tears.

"Finneas, where on earth have you been? I thought that you were killed in battle."

"I am so sorry, Mammy," Finneas said as he ran into the warmth of his mother's open arms.

"Never mind. You are here now and that is all that matters. Let me get you something to eat, son."

Finneas sat at the table and watched as his mother went over to the stove and placed some hot porridge into a bowl. The fire was blazing in the hearth despite the heat outside. A statue of St Anthony was on the mantelpiece beside a porcelain dog. Kathleen took off her straw hat and placed it on the table.

"Where did you go last night?" May asked.

Finneas looked at his mother and sister. How could he possibly tell them what happened? They would never believe him.

"I went with Cara to the hospital. Then I had to give a girl a lift home on my horse."

"What girl?" His mother stared at him.

"She is called Síofra. You wouldn't know her. She lives near Soul Shadow Manor."

"But that's miles away, Finneas."

"I know, Ma. But she had no other way of getting home."

"Does Síofra have white hair?" Kathleen asked.

"Yes, Kathleen, she does. How do you know?"

"I saw her once with Cara."

"Yes, she's her friend. I must go to check on Cara as soon as I have my breakfast."

Kathleen stood up and placed her hand on her brother's arm.

215

"Oh Finneas, haven't you heard?" she said with tears in her eyes.

"Heard what?" Finneas dropped his spoon and it fell onto the floor. He stood up and looked at his mother who was dabbing her eyes with a handkerchief.

"Cara passed away last night, Finneas."

"I don't believe you! The doctor told me that she would survive!"

"That's what they thought, Finneas. But when the surgeon operated on her he found that the bullet was too close to her heart. There was nothing anyone could do. They've taken her home to Daphney Castle."

"No!" Tears fell from Finneas's eyes. "How could this happen? It can't be true."

He ran to the door.

"Wait, Finneas, come back! Where are you going?" May cried.

"I am going to Daphney Castle. I won't believe that Cara is dead until I see her with my own two eyes."

"Can I come with you, Finneas?" Kathleen asked.

"No, Kathleen. I must go alone. Can you stay here and take care of Mammy for me until I return?"

"Yes, Finneas, I will. Don't worry."

Finneas smiled at her. "Good girl." He kissed Kathleen on the head.

May placed her hand on her heart. "Take care out there, son. The Redcoats are everywhere. Now that they have won the battle, they think that they own the town."

"I will be careful, Mammy, I promise."

Finneas ran out onto the Island road. People were standing in doorways, huddled like flocks of crows, discussing the battle of Vinegar Hill and mourning for the loss of their loved ones. Finneas suddenly felt scared. He realised that Síofra really was a banshee. Her cry must have caused Cara's death. As he climbed back on his horse, one question ran like a river through his mind. What if he was next?

Chapter twenty-four

THE STILLNESS OF THE SWAN

Finneas was not prepared for the sadness and grief that awaited him at Daphney Castle. People he recognised had gathered to pay their respects. He spied Kitty carrying a bouquet of roses into the castle.

"Kitty!" he cried.

Kitty turned around to see who was calling her name. She was dressed from head to toe in black. Her eyes were swollen from crying.

"Finneas, it's you. Thank God you are alive." A small smile flickered like candlelight across her lips. Seeing Finneas and his large blue eyes was like sunshine bursting through the clouds on a stormy day.

"Is it true, Kitty? Is Cara really dead?"

Kitty sighed. "Yes, Finneas, it is true. Where is Síofra?"

"She is hiding at Soul Shadow Manor."

"Would you like to come inside and pay your respects?"

Finneas turned pale. "No, Kitty. I would rather stay outside."

"It's alright, Finneas. I will be there with you and Cara looks so peaceful."

"Alright then." Finneas nodded and followed Kitty inside.

"She is in the library."

Finneas followed Kitty into the library. The place where only a day ago he had drunk milk and eaten biscuits. His heart sank as he recalled Cara's smile. The piano had been moved and in its place was a large bed with a gold frame.

Finneas gathered himself together. He knew that he must be brave. He clenched his fists and glanced over at the bed where Cara lay. Her right hand was folded across her chest. Her wing stretched across the pillow. She looked like an angel. Finneas reached out his hand and touched the smooth white feathers. Cara was wearing a blue dress with black leather boots. It looked as though she was dressed for a party. All around her were yellow and pink roses. She reminded Finneas of a princess from a fairy tale. Before he knew what was happening his bottom lip trembled. His shoulders shook and tears fell from his eyes.

Kitty walked over to him. She held his hand and led him to a large armchair in the corner of the room.

"Somebody open the window. The boy needs some air! And fetch a glass of water. He has had a terrible shock."

Finneas recalled his mother's words when his father died: *"Grief is a powerful force. It is like the wind, Finneas. It can knock you from your feet and not everyone can stand back up again."*

Suddenly Finneas felt a hand on his left shoulder. He turned his head and saw Mr O'Leary standing there, with his arm in a sling. Tears were gathered in the corner of his eyes.

"The hospital told us that you were the person who brought Cara in."

"Yes, sir."

"Please call me Séamus."

Finneas smiled and looked down at the floor.

"We are glad to hear that Cara had a friend to take care of her."

"It was my pleasure."

Kitty handed Finneas a glass of water which he gulped down.

Mr O'Leary walked over to the window.

"What I don't understand, Finneas, is why Cara was on Vinegar Hill in the first place. And where is that girl she rescued from the sea?"

Finneas felt like a deer standing before a hunter. He hadn't for one minute expected all of these questions. He flashed a look at Kitty, who stepped forward.

"Pardon, sir, but Finneas looks exhausted. He has had a long night. Maybe you could ask him these questions later?"

"This is none of your business, Kitty. Send Spellfinder in, will you?"

Mr O'Leary's words pricked Kitty like a thorn on a rose. She gave Finneas a pitying look and ran from the room.

Moments later Spellfinder bounded in. Kitty walked behind her like a shadow.

"You asked for me, sir?"

"Ah, Spellfinder, yes. Finneas has called to pay his respects. He was the boy who brought Cara to the hospital."

"I see, sir."

"I was just asking him what on earth Cara was

doing at the battle of Vinegar Hill when I strictly forbade it."

"I don't know, sir," Finneas replied truthfully. "All that I know is that I saw her there with Síofra."

"Ah yes, Síofra. Spellfinder, tell us what people in the town are saying about Síofra, will you?"

Spellfinder bowed her head. "They are saying that she is a banshee, sir. That she came from Banshee Island to take the souls of the dead back with her. People say that she cursed the battle and that is why we lost. They are also saying ..."

"Go on, Spellfinder, out with it!"

"They are also saying that she is to blame for Cara's death."

Finneas jumped up. His eyes grew wide with fright.

"No. You are wrong. Síofra loved Cara – she would not do anything to hurt her."

Séamus O'Leary and Spellfinder looked at each other in disbelief.

"You're not defending her, are you, Finneas?"

"Yes, I mean no, sir."

Finneas did not know what to do or who to believe. Síofra had told him herself that she was a banshee. He had seen her kill the toad with his own two eyes. Could he really trust her? For all he knew Síofra could be making it all up. Suddenly the room started to spin. He gripped the back of the chair to steady himself, but it was no use. His knees buckled beneath him and he fell to the ground with an almighty thud. The last thing he heard was Kitty's scream.

Chapter twenty-five

THE HOME OF THE SWAN-GIRL

Síofra slept soundly in Cara's old bed. It felt strange to be in Cara's room without her. She awoke to the sound of birdsong. She crept from the four-poster bed and went out onto the balcony. There were birds everywhere in the trees and on the roof. It was then that she recalled Cara's wing. Of course, the birds would love to be close to her. She was after all part-bird part-girl.

A tattered old raven flew through the air and landed on Síofra's shoulder. "You miss her, too, don't you, boy?" she whispered to the bird, who pecked at her hand with its beak.

The sun had risen hours ago. It hung like a large orange in the sky. A gentle breeze blew the curtains,

Síofra observed the spot where Banshee Island stood. It was barely visible. She knew that it wouldn't be long until the island would vanish for good. It was hard to believe that a few days ago, Cara stood in this very same spot looking at her, longing to be by her side. So much had happened since then.

Síofra walked back into the bedroom and shut the balcony windows. Then she walked over to Cara's wardrobe and opened it. There were so many beautiful dresses. Each one had been adapted for her wing. How sad it was that Cara was ashamed to have feathers instead of an arm.

"Oh, Cara, I wish you were here!" Síofra cried.

Then she walked over to the dressing table, where hours earlier she had left *The Book of Dark and Scary Folktales*. She sat on the chair and flicked through the pages. Something told her that this book meant something. She had already discovered that the tale of the Green Man was true. Could it be possible that the other dark and scary folktales were true also? Then there was the page that fell out with the picture of the street organ. What did it mean? It was then she noticed something else. There was a beautiful illustration on page forty of a woman who had wings instead of arms, just like Cara. She was on Banshee Island. Síofra gasped as she read the story of *The Astonishing Flight of Children with Wings*. The words danced before her eyes. Long before banshees lived there, the island belonged to a beautiful colony of swans. One of the swans fell in love with a man. She longed to be human so she asked a witch to cast a spell. She gave up her wonderful song and swapped her wings for arms. Suddenly Síofra knew the truth. Cara's mother and Banshee Island was her true home. Síofra realised that Cara longed for the island, just as she longed to be close to her. Her heart beat in her chest. This explained everything. Síofra recalled the two golden swans who still lived on the island. They must have been related to Cara somehow.

The sound of footsteps on the stairs alerted Síofra to danger. Voices swam through the air.

"She must be here somewhere!"

"No!" Siofra gasped as she realised that Mr Crooks had come for her. Finneas must have betrayed her trust. A single tear fell from her eye. "I thought he was my friend," she whispered.

The door burst open and seven little girls wearing masks led a procession of people over to Síofra.

The angry mob grabbed her arms and legs and carried her kicking and screaming out of the manor.

They threw her onto the back of a wooden cart.

Crooks sat next to her. "You thought you had got away from us. But there is no escape. Tonight as the moon rises in the sky, the Green Man will rise. We will hunt you down. You will have to run for your life. If we find you we will break your bones. If the Green Man finds you first you will become a Booley Girl and stay lost forever."

Chapter twenty-six

THE WICKED BIRDS

When Finneas woke up, he was lying on a table in Doyle's Barn. Candles were lit and seven small girls in masks stood around him chanting the ancient curse.

We are seven
seven are we
friends forever
forever we will be
alone on the mountains
singing our song,
green mist descended
everything went wrong,
so come up and find us
if you dare

The Booley Girls of Wexford
will meet you there.

There were other people too. All of them were wearing masks and costumes in preparation for the Green Man Festival. The seven girls clapped hands and skipped. It made a frightening sight.

Finneas wondered for a moment where he was. Then he remembered seeing Cara, talking to Mr O'Leary and fainting. Someone must have carried him out of Daphney Castle and put him on the table in Doyle's Barn.

Suddenly Spellfinder appeared. She beckoned one of the young girls.

"You can take off your mask now, Kathleen."

Kathleen did as she was told.

"Hello, Finneas," Kathleen said. Then she smiled to reveal a gap in her teeth.

Finneas sat bolt upright. His head throbbed. He could not believe his eyes.

"Kathleen, what on earth are you doing here?"

"I told you, Finneas. I am a Booley Girl."

"Go home right away, Kathleen! You are not to have anything to do with this silly Green Man Festival, do you hear me? It's not safe here. These people can't be trusted. Run as fast as you can!"

The crowd of masked spectators gasped. Then they hissed and booed at Finneas.

Spellfinder scowled. "How dare you, Finneas Pepper! You think you are better than us, always meddling in things that don't concern you. Your father was the same."

"You leave my father out of it. He is dead and can't defend himself."

"He tried to put a stop to the Green Man Festival once before, you know. Long before you were born. He came up here and told us we were all superstitious fools."

"He was right."

"Is that so, Finneas Pepper? Did you know that it was your great-great-great-grandfather that made the Death Coach for the Green Man? I suppose you could say that your ancestors are partly to blame for the disappearance of the Booley Girls all those years ago. That makes you responsible too."

Finneas flashed a look at Kathleen. "What are you waiting for, Kathleen? Go home and tell Ma to get help."

Kathleen nodded, then turned to run but Spellfinder gripped her wrist. Kathleen screamed.

Finneas jumped off the table.

"Let her go!"

"I can't do that, Finneas. Your sister is dressed up as one of the Booley Girls so we need her tonight."

"Kathleen has nothing to do with any of this, you wicked witch!"

"How dare you speak to me like that, you insolent boy. Kathleen has been quite helpful to us, Finneas. She told us where to find your young banshee friend."

"No, that's a lie!" Finneas ran over to his sister and pulled her free from Spellfinder's grip. "Kathleen has no idea where Síofra is."

Tears fell from Kathleen's eyes. "Oh, Finneas. I am so sorry. You told me that Síofra was at Soul Shadow Manor, and I told Mrs Spellfinder. How will you ever forgive me?"

Finneas realised that he should never have told Kathleen where Síofra was. It was a foolish mistake, and one that could cost them their lives, but he knelt down in front of his sister and looked directly into her eyes. "Never mind all that now, Kathleen. It's not your fault. Síofra will be well gone by now – she'll be alright."

"No, she's on her way, Finneas. Mr Crooks and some of the others have gone to fetch her."

"You foolish girl! You are in big trouble, do you hear me?" Mrs Spellfinder screeched. Then she reached out to grab Kathleen.

Finneas jumped up and pushed Spellfinder. She fell backwards and hit her head off a wooden chair.

The crowd were outraged. They gathered around and helped Mrs Spellfinder to her feet.

"You stupid boy!" she spat. "You will pay for this. Don't you understand? We need Síofra so that we can start the Green Man Hunt. She was the chosen one. If we don't hunt her today, then the whole town will be cursed. The Booley Girls will come back from the dead. They will take her to join them instead of one of us. Perhaps we should hunt your sister instead."

"*No!*" Kathleen screamed. "*Please, Finneas, please don't let them hunt me!*"

Kathleen threw her arms around her brother's neck.

Finneas whispered in her ear. "I won't let them hunt you, Kathleen. I promise. But you need to get home to Mammy as soon as possible and stay there until I come home. Do you understand me? Make sure that she has placed the eggshells on the doorstep, to stop the hunt from entering our house."

"Yes, Finneas."

"Good girl. I will distract this mob, so you can go."

He unwound her arms from around his neck and stood up.

"*Where is Síofra?*" Finneas shouted, then he pushed

his way through the angry crowd. *"Let me see her! What have you done with her?"*

"All in good time. You will see her soon enough!" Mrs Spellfinder yelled after him.

Finneas turned to shout back at her. *"I want to see her now!"* He breathed a sigh of relief as he saw Kathleen running off down the mountain.

A group of the spectators surrounded him. They wore crow masks and reminded Finneas of plague doctors. Their masks had large beaks that protruded from the centre of their faces. Slick feathers were sewn onto their ragged brown costumes. Their heads were bent as they flapped their makeshift wings and for a moment Finneas thought that the wicked birds were about to take flight.

Chapter twenty-seven

THE HUNT FOR THE GREEN MAN

"Let me go!" Síofra shouted as the horse and cart trundled along the narrow roads that led up the Blackstairs Mountain.

She was not alone on the back of the cart. There were two men with wolf masks beside her. Síofra felt sorry for the wolves that were killed so that these men could make ridiculous costumes out of their skin. The dead wolves' jaws opened to reveal mouthfuls of sharp teeth. One of the men was playing the flute; the other man banged a drum and sang a song. Crooks held the reins.

It was a warm day. Fields of golden flowers were filled with butterflies. Further up the mountain the fields transformed to purple heather. Síofra glanced around, desperately looking for places that she could hide, when later darkness descended she would be hunted on the mountainside. It was impossible to take it all in. There was a thought that kept thrashing around inside her head, like a boat in a storm. "What if I never get home to Banshee Island again?" Síofra had seen with her own two eyes how the island looked as though it could disappear at any moment. She might never see Silver again or guide the souls of the dead to the afterlife. She should never have come to the Land of the Living. It was all her fault that Cara was in the battle of Vinegar Hill and that Finneas was caught up in all of this.

Síofra knew that people would travel from villages all around for the hunt. She wondered if the Green Man would appear to her. I need to be brave, she said to herself.

The rhythmic movement of the cart and the sound of the man singing, combined with her exhaustion, sent Síofra into a deep sleep and she did not wake until they arrived at Doyle's Barn. The sun had sunk low in the sky. The heat from earlier had been replaced by a chill breeze. Síofra couldn't believe her eyes. An enormous crowd of people had gathered. People had travelled from villages all across Carlow and Wexford. They want to rid the land of the Curse of the Booley Girls.

"*There she is!*" a man cried.

"*The banshee is here – we are all doomed!*"

"Don't look directly in her eyes," a barefooted woman in a red shawl warned her children. "Just one look from her and you will drop stone dead."

Síofra noticed that the people were all wearing green. Their masks and gloves made a terrifying sight. A woman in a donkey costume threw a stone and it hit Síofra's shoulder. Another person spat at her. Síofra longed to cry, but she held it in. She knew that there was power in her tears. If she cried, she could kill someone. Síofra realised that the people were all scared of her. They had never seen a banshee before.

They began to chant the song of the Booley Girls.

We are seven
seven are we
friends forever
forever we will be
alone on the mountains
singing our song,
green mist descended
everything went wrong,
so come up and find us

if you dare
The Booley Girls of Wexford
will meet you there.

It looked as though they were all in a trance. The smell of smoke travelled up Síofra's nostrils. Then she saw a spectacular fire. Orange and yellow flames danced against the black sky. The huge straw Green Man was burning on the mountaintop. People could see him from miles around. Síofra's legs shook. Her teeth chattered. What if she was next? What if they come for her when the straw giant had turned to dust. Girls in green and white dresses were dancing around a maybush that was decorated with eggshells. Boys wearing masks that resembled goats' heads joined them. The girls carried straw dollies. They held them up in the air and span in circles.

It was then that Síofra spotted Finneas. His was the only face without a mask. Her heart thumped. Why was he there? Was Finneas one of them? Did he want her dead too? No, he didn't.

Finneas pushed his way through the crowd. Síofra saw him and smiled. His elbows were like oars parting waves. "Let me through!" he cried. Then he was within arms' reach.

Suddenly Spellfinder was there. She gripped

Finneas by the wrist and pulled him back.

"Not so fast, lad!" the wicked woman shouted.

Suddenly a horn was blown. The sound was deafening and it silenced the crowd. The two men in the wolf masks gripped Síofra by the arms. They lifted her high in the air. Then they placed her on the makeshift stage beside Spellfinder while others held Finneas back.

"We have waited for this moment for a long time. Thirty years ago the Booley Girls vanished from this mountainside. Seven young girls, came up here to milk their cows. They churned butter and sang songs. Until the Green Man stole them away. A curse was placed upon our land. Each year a person is selected by a young girl to be the next person to be hunted. We offer the person's soul to the Booley Girls. Tonight we have a very special person. Allow me to present Síofra to you!"

People whispered to each other in the darkness.

"As you can see from her white hair, Síofra is no ordinary girl. Are you, Síofra?"

"Please, I am begging you all to let me go!"

"Not until you tell the good people who you are."

"No, I won't do it." Síofra remembered what Silver had said to her. Never tell anyone that you are a banshee. How could she have been so foolish as to let them see she was?

Spellfinder dug her long nails into Síofra's wrist.

"*Ouch!*" Siofra shouted.

Then she realised that she might as well tell the angry mob who she was, as she was going to be hunted to her death and there was nothing she could do about it.

"*I am a banshee!*" she blurted out.

People gasped and cried out.

"I told you!" a woman in a straw dress said to a man dressed as a clown. He wore a pointy hat and had a sinister smile painted on his face.

"*Let her go! She doesn't know what she is saying!*" Finneas bounded up onto the stage and pulled Síofra away from Spellfinder.

"What have we here?" Mr Crooks said as he joined them. "I think, ladies and gentlemen, that someone else wants to take Síofra's place. Is that right, young Finneas?"

Finneas gulped and swallowed down his fear. He had to be brave. Síofra needed his help. He promised Cara that he would take care of her and it was a promise that he intended to keep.

"No, it is not right. I don't want any part in the

Green Man Festival. I just want you to let Síofra go."

"You must all excuse the behaviour of young Finneas Pepper. We received some very sad news today. I am so sorry to say that young Cara O'Leary was killed at the Battle of Vinegar Hill."

Síofra could not believe her ears. It was a lie. It had to be. Surely she would know if Cara was dead? They were connected. As close as sisters. She loved Cara with all her heart. She glanced at Finneas. Tears fell from his eyes. He bowed his head in sorrow. Síofra realised that what Spellfinder said was true. Cara was dead. Her best friend was gone forever. She should have been there to help her. Instead she may have killed her. Blood pumped through Síofra's veins. The earth beneath them all shook and trembled. She held her hands up in the air and then she roared.

People screamed and ran for cover as rocks tumbled down the mountainside and the ground cracked open like an egg beneath their feet.

Síofra's eyes flashed emerald green. It's all my fault, she thought. I killed the only friend I have ever had.

Then another scream pierced the night air like scissors cutting through silk.

"Mr Crooks has dropped dead!"

A woman cradled Mr Crooks in her arms.

People buzzed around like flies, not knowing what to do.

Spellfinder grabbed one of the musician's horns and sounded it.

"On this night may the Booley Girls rise and the young girl's fate will be decided. *Count to ten and then give chase. The hunt will begin, let us all make haste!*"

Síofra jumped off the back of the stage. Finneas ran towards her.

"Which way, Finneas?"

"Follow me. We have ten seconds before they come after us."

They ran further up the mountainside.

"Should we not go down the mountain?"

"No, Síofra. That is what they will expect us to do."

Three words thumped in Síofra's head. *Cara is dead.* Grief wrapped itself around her throat like a snake, strangling her. *Cara is dead.*

They ran through clumps of purple heather. Jumped over boulders and rocks. "*Ouch!*" Síofra cried as she caught her arm on a bramble and the thorns tore at her skin.

"Are you alright?"

"Yes, Finneas – don't stop – we don't have long!" Síofra knew that she had to survive this night. She needed to get home to Banshee Island. Or else it was all for nothing. The sound of dogs barking and drums banging loudly told them that the hunt was under way.

"Where are we going?"

"To the top of the mountain."

"Why are we going there?"

"It's the spot they say the Booley Girls haunt. You don't believe in the curse, do you, Síofra?"

"Yes, Finneas, I do and you should too."

"We are coming for you, Banshee!"

"Quickly, Síofra. We have to move fast."

They tumbled over ditches. Trampled on ferns and brambles. Until a dark cloud cast a shadow on the landscape.

"Finneas, look!" Síofra pointed up at the sky. She could not believe her eyes. Hundreds of birds were somersaulting through the clouds. Their feathers were slick and black, their sharp beaks pointing straight ahead. The sound of birdsong filled the air. It drowned out the sound of the hunt.

"I have never seen so many birds together before, Finneas. What do you think it means?"

"I'm sure it doesn't mean anything."

"The birds are following us." Síofra closed her eyes and thought of Cara, of the beautiful white wing that stretched out from her shoulder blade. Her heart soared as she recalled the beautiful birds who used to swim beneath the sea around Banshee Island.

Suddenly the birds changed direction.

"What are they doing now?" she shouted.

It was hard for Finneas to hear her above the cacophony of birdsong. He pulled her sleeve.

"Síofra, we must keep going."

"Finneas, look!"

Finneas turned his head skywards and was mesmerised as he realised that the birds had formed the shape of a swan with its arms outstretched in the sky.

"It's Cara, I know it is," said Síofra. "She is watching over us."

"Quick, Síofra, they are catching up with us."

They ran passed a white hawthorn bush and suddenly a thick fog emerged from the earth beneath their feet.

"Oh, no!" Finneas stopped. "What will we do now? The fog is thick. We won't be able to see where we are going."

"That means that the hunt won't be able to find us either."

"This way. The top of the mountain is right here."

Síofra could not believe her eyes, it was the spot

where she saw the Booley Girls, when she left Cara's carriage.

"I have been here before, Finneas. Or at least I think I have."

Síofra realised that it had all gone quiet. There were no more drums banging or dogs barking. They had made it. They were safe for at least a short while. Hidden in the thick, dense fog.

"Finneas, can you hear the hunt?"

"No, I think we have lost them." A large grin appeared on Finneas's lips.

Síofra was grateful to have Finneas by her side.

Then he grabbed her hard by the forearm. "Síofra! There is someone over there. Behind that tree."

"I can't see anything."

"Look. Where the mist has cleared – right over there. It's a girl."

Síofra gasped. It was the same girl that she saw the last time that she was lost on the mountainside.

"It's one of the Booley Girls, Finneas."

"Nonsense, Síofra. It's probably just a girl who went on the hunt and got lost. Let's go over to her. Perhaps she needs help."

"Finneas, wait. She might get a fright. Perhaps she will think we are ghosts."

"Nonsense, Síofra, how can we be ghosts? The Booley Girls haunt this place, not us. I will get to the bottom of this once and for all."

Finneas strode through the mist to where the girl stood.

Chapter twenty-eight

THE BOOLEY GIRLS FROM WEXFORD

Síofra hid behind a hawthorn bush. The mist was so thick that she couldn't see where she was. She stretched out her hands and they landed on something. It was a creature. A living thing, with horns on top of its skull. She ran her hand down along its neck and down along its hairy body. Her fingers rested on hooves.

"The Green Man!" she screamed.

Then the fog parted momentarily to reveal a black mountain goat. Síofra stared into the animal's eyes. Then she turned and ran in the direction that Finneas went.

"Finneas, where are you?" she shouted.

"I am here."

Síofra followed the sound of Finneas's voice. She found him standing talking to a girl in a yellow headscarf, with large blue eyes and long dark eyelashes. She wore a red dress that flowed down to her ankles and a blue shawl covered her shoulders.

"Síofra, I would like you to meet Ellen."

"Are you a ghost?" Ellen asked Síofra.

"No, Ellen. I am not a ghost. I am a friend."

She was relieved that Ellen could see her. However, it did not explain what was happening.

"Are you part of the hunt, Ellen?" Finneas asked.

"I don't know anything about a hunt. My friends and I came up here for the summer, with our cows. However, this summer didn't end and we can't find our way back home. It feels like we have been up here in the mist forever."

"*Lost in the Mists of Time,*" Síofra whispered.

The green mist danced around them as they spoke. It swirled around their ankles and climbed up their legs.

"What year is it, Ellen?" Finneas asked.

"It's 1768, of course."

Finneas's eyes opened wide in shock. Síofra was right. Ellen was one of the Booley Girls. But how could that be?

Síofra could see the look of distress in the young girl's eyes.

"And you have tried to get home, Ellen?" she asked.

"Yes, we all have. However, every time we do we find ourselves back here."

"How awful for you!"

"There must be some way we can help," Finneas chipped in.

The mist rose until it covered their legs.

"Quick!" said Ellen. "It is not safe here. We need to get back to the others. They are coming soon."

"Who is coming?" Síofra asked, although deep down she already knew the answer to her question.

"The Green Man and his wife. They torment us every night. We have to get inside the Booley Hut quickly. Follow me!"

Ellen led the way and Finneas stepped closer to Síofra.

"I don't understand what is happening."

"We have found the Booley Girls, Finneas."

"But we *can't* have. They disappeared thirty years ago. Spellfinder is playing a trick on us."

Síofra reached out and held Finneas's hand.

"This isn't a trick, Finneas. We seem to have found

ourselves in the Mists of Time. You heard Ellen – she said the year in 1768."

"That was thirty years ago, Síofra."

"Yes, it was."

"What about the Curse of the Booley Girls? They could be dangerous."

"I thought that you didn't believe in superstitions, Finneas?"

"I didn't, I mean I don't."

"That curse was made up – the Booley Girls won't hurt us. Do they look dangerous to you?"

Síofra pointed at the group of terrified young girls huddled together near a fire by a small stone hut.

They leapt to their feet as Ellen ran up to them. Some of them hugged her.

"Ellen, where have you been? We were worried sick about you," a tall girl with wavy brown hair said.

"Don't worry, Bláthnaid, I am safe."

Another of the girls started to scream when Finneas and Síofra appeared through the mist. The others huddled together.

"It's alright, Maeve. Don't scream. This boy and girl were out looking for us. They are going to help us find our way home. They are our friends."

"My name is Deirdre. I am the eldest of the girls. We

have been lost on this mountain forever. We have walked for miles and we just end up back at the same spot. How can you help us? Do you have a map?"

Finneas looked at Síofra and shrugged his shoulders.

"I am sorry, Deirdre, but there is no map that will help you to find your way through the Mists of Time," Síofra said.

"Then we are stuck here forever!" Maeve cried.

Síofra placed her hand on Maeve's arm. "No, Maeve. Not if we can help it. I know of another way."

Bláthnaid's blue shawl fell from her shoulders as she stepped forward. "Please tell us what it is. I would do anything to get off this mountain."

Síofra sighed. "The only way that we can escape is by defeating the Green Man."

The girls gasped and clutched at each other.

"No! We can't!" said Bláthnaid. "There is no way that we can defeat him. He has already taken Róisín from us. He will never set us free."

Finneas scratched his head. "The Green Man must have a weakness. Just like everyone else. All we have to do is find out what that weakness is." He said it as though it was the most obvious thing in the world.

Síofra smiled as he spoke. Then she threw her arms around his neck. "Yes, Finneas, you are right. And I know exactly what his weakness is. But I will need some time to prepare."

"*Oh no!*" Maeve cried. "*I hear the wheels of the Death Coach. He is coming!*"

"Quick, everyone get into the Booley Hut!" Bláthnaid ordered.

The Booley Girls all ran into the small stone hut.

Finneas turned to Síofra who was standing, waiting for the Death Coach to arrive. She had her hands on her hips and a determined look on her face.

"Síofra! We have to hide now!" He grabbed Síofra's wrist and pulled her into the hut.

Then Deirdre rolled a huge stone in front of the entrance.

Síofra's heart was thumping inside her chest as she sat beside Finneas.

"What did you think you were doing out there, Síofra?" Finneas whispered. "You nearly got us both killed."

"I am sorry, Finneas. Truly I am."

Not a shard of light could be seen in the stone hut. The air was cold and damp. The sound of horse's hooves announced the Death Coach's arrival. The Booley Girls held each other's hands and uttered prayers.

Finneas sat trembling beside Síofra.

"I know that you are in there!" The sound of the Green Man's voice pierced the silence.

Síofra's blood rushed through her veins. Her fear of the Green Man was replaced with anger. How dare he take her mother away from her? What right did he have to scare these poor girls for the last thirty years?

Síofra made a silent promise to the Green Man. Tomorrow night, when you come up this mountainside on your Death Coach, I will be waiting for you, Father, just you wait and see. It was a promise that she intended to keep.

Chapter twenty-nine

THE SOUL DANCER'S RETURN

Silver stood on the verge of a golden river. The ancient hawthorn tree exploded like moonlight through the earth. The branches were decorated with dazzling coloured ribbons hung by every soul that arrived to remind them of precious moments from their life.

Silver tried to push thoughts of Síofra from her mind as she awaited the arrival of the new soul, although it was no use. *"Please come home, Síofra!"* she cried and a silver tear fell from her eye. Síofra only had one more day left to return. After that Banshee Island would be gone. Objects had been arriving on the shore for several days now. There was a pair of silver binoculars, a gold ring with a swan engraved on it and beautiful white feathers. Silver had collected them and carefully placed them in the Spectacular Library of Magical Things.

It was then that she saw her walking through the forest. An extraordinary girl with long black hair. Silver gasped. She noticed an astonishing thing. The girl had a wing instead of an arm. Like the girl Síofra had described. The girl from Soul Shadow Manor. A look of confusion crossed the girl's face. It was the same look that all the souls had when they first arrived on Banshee Island.

Tears fell from Silver's eyes as she ran to great her.

"Where I am?" the girl enquired.

"You are safe now."

"I feel as though I have been here before. I recognise this place. Yet I can't remember what I was doing here."

"Don't worry, child. It will take a while for your mind to adjust." Silver was mesmerised by the girl's wing. She had not seen anything like her. Not since the Soul Dancers left. Silver sighed as she recalled the Shapeshifting Swans who had their song stolen from them.

Cara tried to piece together everything that happened. However, everything seemed hazy. It felt as though she was dreaming. She recalled standing on the shore at Soul Shadow Manor and looking across the water at a girl with white hair. Then a name flashed through her mind.

"*Síofra!*" The word leapt out of her mouth, like a frog from a rock pool.

Silver placed her hands on Cara's shoulders.

"Cara, you know my niece?"

"Yes. I mean no. I am not sure."

Images flashed through Cara's mind. A girl on a boat wearing a pirate hat. Another of the same girl holding a fox cub in her arms. Then the girl was swinging on a rope swing. Of course she knew Síofra. She was her best friend. Cara loved her with all her heart. She could never forget her. Not ever. Tears streamed from her eyes. There was a battle. A gun fired and Síofra was crying. Then people were chasing her.

"What is it?"

"This is Banshee Island, isn't it?"

Silver nodded. "Yes, it is. And you are the girl from Soul Shadow Manor. Síofra's friend."

"Yes. My name is Cara."

Silver gulped back her tears.

"You are very welcome here, Cara."

Then she reached into her bag and took out two red ribbons.

"I have a gift for you. But first I must take your full name."

"My name is Cara O'Leary."

"In giving me your name, you are taking the first step towards leaving the Land of the Living behind you."

Silver handed Cara the first ribbon, which Cara tied to a low branch on the old oak tree.

Cara smiled. "Once I went on an incredible journey across the sea, with a girl dressed like a pirate. She ate seaweed snacks and we decided to go on a journey together that would change us forever."

An image of Síofra laughing as she pretended to be a Warrior Queen sparkled in the air.

Silver smiled then she handed Cara another ribbon which she tied to a branch further up the tree.

"I have a memory of a girl in her grandmother's cottage, telling me that she thought I was beautiful." Another image of Síofra was projected up into the sky, a huge smile beaming across her lips, like a rainbow after a storm.

Silver realised that Cara was sharing those memories with her to make her happy.

"Thank you, Cara."

"Síofra told me that the souls who arrive on this

island travel on the back of a swan to the otherworld."

"Yes, Cara, that is true. However, I don't feel as though that path is for you. It is not your time to leave here yet."

Silver took her purple hat off. She plucked the feather that had belonged to one of the Soul Dancers from the brim of her hat. Then she handed it to Cara. "This feather will tell us everything that we need to know."

"How?"

"Just wait and see, Cara."

Moments later the feather felt hot in Cara's hand. Then it started to change before their eyes. Silver and Cara watched in amazement. The feather had turned to gold.

"It is just as I thought. You belong to the ancient race of Soul Dancers who once lived on Banshee Island."

"I have heard of them before. But you must be mistaken, Silver. I only have one wing. I couldn't possibly be a Soul Dancer. I am neither bird or human."

"My dearest child, you are perfect exactly as you are. The feather only changes to gold when put into the hand of a real Soul Dancer."

A smile danced a jig across Cara's lips. She finally felt as though she belonged.

"How did you hear about the Soul Dancers, Cara?"

"I always knew that my mother was a shape-shifting swan. However, when I was here with Síofra she showed me *The Book of Dark and Scary Folktales from Long Ago*. I read the story about the swans who used to live on Banshee Island. It was then that I understood why I felt connected to Banshee Island. It is because this is my true home."

"Yes, it is, Cara. I have been trying for years to work out how to find the song that the witches took from the Soul Dancers. I truly believe that if I find the song that the soul-dancing swans will return to Banshee Island."

"Perhaps this could help you."

Cara reached into her pocket and pulled out the watercolour illustration that fell from the pages of *The Book of Dark and Scary Folktales from Long Ago*.

Silver gasped at the sight of the astonishing picture. She recognised what it was straight away. It was a remarkable musical street organ on huge cast-iron wheels. Large gold clay swans with outstretched wings adorned the side of it. The swans' wings flapped whenever the instrument was played. It was extravagantly decorated in silver. However, in the centre of the organ was a large gold clockwork heart, with a key inside it. All you had to do was turn the key to hear the music. The street organ was ancient. In the olden days, it was played by an organ grinder who pushed the magical organ around the streets of towns and cities in Ireland. However, it arrived on the island over a hundred years ago when the organ grinder died, along with The Book of Scary Folktales from Long Ago.

"This is extraordinary, Cara. This fantastic musical instrument is in the Spectacular Library of Magical Things. However, I don't understand why you are showing it to me."

"Turn over the page and all may be revealed."

Silver smiled at Cara as she turned the page over. There was a message that had been written with a quill and ink. It was waiting to be read.

Silver gasped as she read the words.

The swan's song is hidden in a heart of gold.

"But whatever could it mean?" asked Cara.

"I think that we may have discovered where the witch hid the Soul Dancers Song, Cara. It must be in the golden heart of the magical street organ."

"Do you think that if we release the song the Soul Dancers will return to Banshee Island?"

"I can't say for certain, Cara. There is only one way to find out."

Silver reached out and took Cara's hand. Together

they hurried through the evergreen forest, past heather and gorse, over tufts of grass and bubbling streams. Then through the gates of a crumbling graveyard until eventually they reached the stone steps that led to the library. Silver smiled at Cara who flapped her wing, then together they hurried up the two hundred stone steps. They knew that the future of the Soul Dancers depended on them.

Chapter thirty

THE REAL DANCE

Golden sunlight cracked like an egg over the mountain. Yet the thick green mist remained. Síofra knew that they didn't have long to prepare. In less than twelve hours the Green Man's Death Coach would be trundling up the mountainside. Síofra was also aware that her plan might not work. She was taking a huge risk. If the plan failed they could all be killed. However, it was their only hope of ever escaping from the Mists of Time and defeating the Green Man once and for all and it was a chance that Síofra was willing to take.

The Booley Girls and Finneas stood in a circle holding hands as Síofra had instructed them to do. Síofra stood in the centre of the circle. She swallowed down her fear. If she wanted the Booley Girls to believe in her then she realised that she would have to appear confident, even if she didn't feel it.

"We are all here now, Síofra. Or at least all except Róisín," Deidre said then she turned her gaze towards the sky.

Síofra walked towards Deirdre and placed her hand on her shoulder. Síofra knew that as the oldest Booley Girl, Deirdre felt the weight of responsibility on her shoulders. If Síofra could get Deirdre to agree to her plan then the others would follow. However, Síofra understood that this might not be as easy as it sounded.

"I am sorry to hear about Róisín, Deirdre. However, she is safe for now."

"How can you be so sure?" Deirdre enquired.

"Because I saw her."

The girls gasped and then turned to each other.

"Where did you see her?" Maeve asked.

"I have a special gift. It's hard to explain, but I can communicate with people who are lost or those who have died."

"I told you she was a witch!" Mary piped up. "We can't trust a witch."

Finneas broke free of the circle and joined Síofra in the centre. He placed his left hand on her shoulder.

"Síofra might be many things, but she is definitely not a witch. Just because she has been born with a special gift doesn't mean that she is wicked."

Síofra smiled at Finneas. She hadn't met many boys before and she hoped that they were all as kind as her friend.

Deirdre frowned. "Finneas is right. Róisín had a gift. She had the cure and could heal those who were sick and she wasn't wicked either. If Síofra said that she saw Róisín and that she is safe then I believe her. Besides we can't give up hope."

"If my plan works then it won't just be us who will be set free. Róisín will escape too."

"What exactly is your plan, Síofra. We need to hear it before we agree to anything."

"Of course, Deirdre. I understand. What I am about to propose may seem strange to you at first. All I ask is that you listen to me."

"You have our full attention," Deirdre replied.

"The Green Man has hooves for feet and horns growing from the side of his head. He has rectangular pupils and a long white beard. Which means that he is as much a goat as he is a man."

"I don't like all this talk about the Green Man. It is scaring me!" Maeve cried.

Bláthnaid put her arm around her friend.

"Please continue, Síofra." Deirdre folded her arms across her chest.

"Goats detest water. They can't stand getting wet. They are petrified of the rain."

Mary tugged her blue shawl around her shoulders. "We haven't seen water on this mountain for as long as I can remember. All that we have is this green mist."

"That's why we need to make it rain," Síofra said.

Finneas tutted. "You know that I believe in you, Síofra, and I would do anything to help you, but there is no way in the world that we can make it rain."

"That is where you are wrong, Finneas. I have seen it done before. Do any of you girls have musical instruments here?"

"I have a harp," Maeve said as she wiped the tears from her eyes with the back of her hand.

"Great, Maeve. Would you mind getting it, please?"

Maeve hitched up her skirt and ran into the Booley Hut.

Deirdre raised her hand. "I have a bodhrán."

"Perfect, Deirdre. The beat of a drum will really help."

Deirdre walked over to the rock where she had been milking the cows earlier. Her bodhrán was next to it.

"What do you want the rest of us to do?" Mary asked.

Síofra took a deep breath. Then she paced up and down as she spoke.

"I come from an island off the coast of Ireland. Each year many people travel there. Sometimes they come from farflung lands."

Síofra had decided not to tell the girls that she was a banshee and that the people who visited her home were the souls of the dead. It would be too much for them to take in and it might frighten them to think that they were alone on the mountainside with a banshee.

"One of the visitors to my island came from an island called Hawai in the Pacific Ocean. She was a young girl who wore a vibrant yellow skirt. She told me that in her land people have the ability to summon the elements. They call on storms, rain and wind. They believe that when they call upon the elements they will come."

Deirdre looked up to the sky. "How do they summon storms?"

"They do it through a dance that mimics the thrashing of the wind and the pounding of the rain. Doing this dance transports them into the realm of their ancestors. Those that came before them. They are

265

connecting with nature. The sun in the sky and the seeds that grow in the earth. They often go up on mountaintops. They chant and ask the rain to fall from the sky."

"It sounds incredible, Síofra," Finneas said.

"I know. But I have seen her do it and she showed me how. More than anything it is a matter of believing you have the power to do it."

Deirdre gazed at Síofra. "It sounds like Séan Nós dancing. We all do it up here. It passes the hours away."

"I can do it too," Finneas said. "My da was great at it. People said that he was so good that he could dance on a sixpence."

Síofra had never heard of it before. Living on Banshee Island meant that she missed out on so many of the pastimes of the young people from the mainland. "Can you explain Séan Nós dancing to me?"

"It is an ancient style of Irish dance," Deirdre explained. "We dance by moving our feet low to the ground while we move our arms freely. There is no set pattern to the dance, Síofra. It is more about self-expression. The freedom to be yourself and to allow the dance to move through you, just like the rain moves through the clouds."

"We can show you, Síofra," Bláthnaid said.

"Yes, you'd better do that."

Síofra had underestimated the Booley Girls. She'd thought that they would be against a dance to summon a storm. However, dancing was part of them, as natural to them as breathing the wild mountain air.

Maeve picked up her harp and began to play. Deirdre joined in with her bodhrán and one by one the rest of the Booley Girls danced. They pounded on the earth with their feet, beating their steps into the ground, where the bones of their ancestors were buried. Dust flew from their heels. The mist swam around their ankles. Leaves rustled like coins in the trees. Then they all joined hands and moved around in a circle.

When their dance was done, Bláthnaid sang *"Eileanóir na Rún"*, an ancient song about a girl from County Wexford. Síofra's heart soared with the sound of the sweet music. She was more determined now than ever to help the Booley Girls to escape.

"We should rest for now. Later at the time when the sun of daytime is replaced in the sky with the moon of night, the Green Man will come up the mountainside and we will summon the storms from the sky. We will call upon the elements to take us home."

Chapter thirty-one

HEART SONG

Cara bounded up the spiral staircase while Silver led the way. Cara was mesmerised by the extraordinary way the staircase coiled its way up the body of a wooden dragon. Silver smiled at Cara when they reached the magical blue door. It was concealed by a trailing foxglove plant.

Silver carefully moved the ancient plant. "Tread carefully, Cara. This plant may look harmless but it is poisonous to humans. Although you are no longer living, I don't want to take any chances."

A cacophony of peculiar sounds and pungent smells seeped from the door. Cara screamed and fell backwards as a flock of one-eyed magpies flew through the air.

"You have met the guardians of the library, Cara."

One of the magpies landed on Cara's wing and Silver smiled. The guardians of The Spectacular Library of Magical things approved of Cara O'Leary. Cara gasped as she stepped through the door. Síofra had told her all about the tremendous and treacherous place which contained the essence of souls that were good and bad.

Silver closed her eyes. Then she raised her hands in the air, as though she were conducting an invisible orchestra and she uttered the words.

"Objects, objects from everywhere.

Show yourselves if you dare.

The Banshee has spoken

Her words have been said

Do not disappoint me

I have spoken to your dead."

A blast of wind gathered and blew Cara's wing like a sail. She grasped the bannister with her right hand. Suddenly it felt as though she was flying. She was horizontal with her two legs pointing out behind her like branches of trees.

Silver held Síofra's banshee's comb in her hand, and shoved it against the door which opened immediately. Silver and Cara were tossed inside by a stormy gust of wind. The door closed behind them with a thud.

Silver recalled bringing Síofra into the library. So much had happened since then. If only Síofra would come home. Silver swallowed her sorrow. She could not help but notice how easily Cara adjusted to being inside The Spectacular Library of Magical Things. She did not need the black spectacles to stop the dizziness that Síofra experienced. It was as though she was born to be there.

Cara peered up at the starlight above her head. She could make out the constellations. The starlight shone down like a million silver coins, held in a black silk purse.

Cara was astounded by the enthralling objects that surrounded her. A jar containing a human heart, an emerald necklace and a dinosaur bone.

"This way, Cara." Silver beckoned.

Cara followed Silver's footsteps. Her right shoulder blade ached. I must have injured it during the battle of Vinegar Hill, she thought. Sadness flowed like a river through her veins. The battle of Vinegar Hill was the last time that she saw Síofra. Cara could not help wondering where her friend was now. If miserable old Spellfinder had her way Síofra would probably be taking part in that stupid Green Man Festival. She prayed that they wouldn't hurt her. Cara would never forgive herself if anything happened to her friend.

"Step carefully, Cara, and take my hand. We have to walk past the dark corner of the library to get to the magical street organ with the golden heart."

Cara gulped. The magical room appeared to shrink as they got closer to the dark corner of the library. Darkness descended. The stench was disgusting and caused Cara to feel sick. She covered her mouth with her wing. Hundreds of flies swarmed through the air. Cara could hardly see where she was going. Thick green sludge oozed from the darkness and stuck to her feet. It was a hideous sight to behold. Síofra told her that it appeared when the Booley Girls went missing thirty years ago. If only there was a way to help them, she thought as she walked over a small, arched wooden bridge.

Silver hurried on ahead. "Quickly, Cara!"

Cara ran after her.

Cara could not believe her eyes. There in the Spectacular Library of Magical Things was the street organ.

Cara pulled the picture from her pocket. "It is identical, Silver. It must be the same one. Although it is even more magnificent in real life." She turned the page over and read the words out loud. *"The swan's song is hidden in a heart of gold."*

There in the centre of the organ was a large gold clockwork heart, with a key inside it. Silver reached out and held Cara's hand.

"This golden heart beats with the voices of your ancestors, Cara. You are a Soul Dancer. One of the true custodians of Banshee Island. You were drawn here for a reason. Just as the birds know how to migrate. You were called to come here. You felt it and Síofra did too. I should have trusted her when she asked to go. I will never doubt her again."

"Síofra is lucky to have you, Silver. Everything that you have done for her is because you care for her. You know it and Síofra does too."

"The time has come for you to turn the key, Cara."

"Do you believe that my mother's song is held within the golden heart?"

"Yes, I do, and you should be the one to set it free."

Chapter thirty-two

THE MISTS OF TIME

A blanket of night carpeted the land. Stars swayed in the sky. Seven girls and one boy gathered on the cold mountainside. They stood in a circle bound together by silver threads of hope. Tonight they would dance through the Mists of Time. They closed their eyes and rummaged through their memories. They imagined running down the mountainside, the wind at their back, the gorse and heather beneath their feet. Thorns and brambles would not stop them. Rocks on the mountainside as old as time itself would greet them on the way down. They would be nimble and light-footed, the smell of smoke from turf fires moving through their nostrils. Candlelight on the window sills in thatched cottages would burn for them. Mothers and fathers would welcome them home.

They braced themselves as the sound of the Death Coach approached. They ignored the instinct to run and hide as a hideous laugh filled the air. Deirdre picked up her bodhrán and banged it as loudly as she could. Maeve's fingers moved effortlessly along the harpstrings as Síofra and Finneas joined the Booley Girls to dance. They pounded their feet against the rocks. Their red skirts twirled like poppies in the sunshine. They whipped up the earth beneath their feet. The Green Man was on the roof of his carriage He circled them, like the green mist that clung to the mountainside. He jumped off and walked towards them. Until he stood in the centre of the circle. Yet they did not look at him, they did not open their eyes, instead they chanted and summon up the elements. They called upon the rain, begged for it to fall on them this night.

We are eight
eight are we
friends forever
forever we will be
alone on the mountains
singing our song,

green mist descended
everything went wrong,
listen to the thunder
the pounding of the rain
The Booley Girls of Wexford
are coming home again.

A single raindrop fell from the sky, then another joined it. Síofra opened her eyes and looked up at the stormcloud overhead. Thunder rumbled and lightning lit up the sky. The wind shook the leaves from the trees and rain fell from the sky.

The Green Man tried to break through the circle but somehow he could not. He was thrown back every time.

The Booley Girls continued their chant. They danced until the earth turned to mud and the rain splashed off the rocks.

We are eight
eight are we
friends forever
forever we will be
alone on the mountains
singing our song,
green mist descended
everything went wrong,

listen to the thunder
the pounding of the rain
The Booley Girls of Wexford
are coming home again.

The Green Man frantically tried to get out of the circle.

"What is happening? Make it stop!" he screamed as torrential rain fell from the sky.

The Booley Girls opened their eyes. They moved towards the Green Man. He fell to his knees and tried to cover his head with his hands but he was no match for the storm that the girls had summoned.

We are eight
eight are we
friends forever
forever we will be
alone on the mountains
singing our song,
green mist descended
everything went wrong,
listen to the thunder
the pounding of the rain,
The Booley Girls of Wexford
are coming home again.

Suddenly the green mist disappeared. The rain

stopped and the moon rose in the sky.

"*Look! He has vanished!*" Maeve shouted.

They all stared at the spot where moments earlier the Green Man lay. However, all that they could see was a giant puddle of murky green water. His clothes floated on top. He had vanished.

They stopped dancing. Deirdre threw her bodhrán onto the ground.

Finneas ran over to Síofra and hugged her in glee. "You did it, Síofra. You saved us all!"

"No, Finneas. We all did it. We all defeated the Green Man. Never again will he have power over us."

He pulled back and stared at her face. "So what's the matter? Why do you look so sad?"

Síofra felt a huge relief that they had defeated the Green Man. However, she could not help but feel sorry for him. He wasn't always bad and regardless of everything that he did, he was her father.

"I just wish that things could have been different, Finneas, that's all."

Finneas placed his hand on her shoulder. "I understand."

A sudden sound alerted the girls to danger.

"*Where are you? We will find you! You can't fool us, Banshee!*"

The Booley Girls huddled together.

"Oh no, Finneas! It is the hunt. I had forgotten all about it. We must go and hide."

"No, Síofra. Tonight you faced your greatest fear. You defeated the Green Man. We will stand together."

The Booley Girls gathered around them.

"Finneas is right, Síofra. We have nothing to fear anymore."

A crowd of people brandishing torches and wearing an assortment of strange straw masks stood in front of them. One person fainted. Another man screamed.

"Deirdre, is that you?" a woman cried and pulled off her mask.

Deirdre was confused at first. The old woman who stood in front of her resembled her mother. Yet she looked so much older. Her long black hair had turned white. Her face was wrinkled. Her back was hunched over. Tears gathered in Deirdre's eyes.

Síofra gripped her hand. "You have all been missing for thirty years. You have stayed the same as you have been trapped in the Mists of Time. However, your families have aged."

"Don't be frightened, Deirdre," the woman said and Deirdre ran into her mother's open arms.

One by one the people on the hunt threw their masks away and welcomed their daughters home.

Spellfinder walked over to Síofra with her head bent. "I owe you an apology. All my life I have lived in fear of the Green Man. I thought that the Booley Girls had cursed us all and that if the hunt did not take place then we would all be doomed. You have shown me that I do not need to live in fear anymore. Thank you for that."

Síofra smiled. She realised that it took great courage for Spellfinder to admit that she was wrong.

"Perhaps we will meet again someday."

"Yes, perhaps we will."

"Are you going back to Daphney Castle?"

"No, Síofra. Now that Cara has gone I don't have a place with that family anymore."

"Where will you go?"

"My sisters will join me soon. We will find a new place to live, I am certain of it," Spellfinder said. The silver hare pendant that she wore around her neck glistened under the moonlight as she turned and walked away.

Síofra watched her go. She could not help but wonder if Spellfinder was a witch.

"That just leaves us then," Finneas said.

"Yes, Finneas. I suppose it does."

"I can see why Cara cared about you, Síofra. You are remarkable."

Síofra could feel the heat rising in her cheeks.

"I couldn't have done any of this without you, Finneas Pepper."

"What will you do now?"

"I have to go home to Banshee Island before it disappears."

"Do you think we will ever meet again, Síofra?"

"Yes, in another seven years when Banshee Island reappears."

"We will be much older then."

"Yes, Finneas. I will be twenty and you will be twenty-one."

"Make sure that you come and find me if you ever come back."

"I will, Finneas, I promise."

Finneas gave Síofra a big hug.

"Goodbye, Síofra."

"Goodbye, Finneas."

Síofra was heartbroken as she watched Finneas run down the mountainside. However, she held back her tears. There was power in them now.

"Síofra! Is that really you?"

Síofra turned around. A beautiful woman stood beside the Death Coach. She was dressed in a green velvet dress. A red cape covered her shoulders. Her skin was pale. Her hair was as white as snow.

"Mother!" Síofra ran into the banshee's open arms. All her life she had dreamed of this moment.

The moon shone down on mother and daughter and they looked into each other's eyes.

"Oh, Síofra! I have missed you. After all these years I am finally going home."

Chapter thirty-three

THE FLUTTER OF WINGS

Cara's hand trembled as she turned the small golden key in the lock. The ache in her shoulder had intensified. Her bones felt as though they had turned to jelly. She twisted the key one more time and an extraordinary thing happened. The most beautiful organ music that Cara had ever heard seeped from the organ pipes. The clay swans flapped their wings feverishly.

"The swan's song is hidden in a heart of gold." Cara's feathers tingled as she said the words out loud.

Suddenly a golden light glowed from the centre of the golden heart and the music was followed by several beautiful voices singing in perfect harmony.

"Cara, look!" Silver pointed above their head.

The starlight glimmered and there flying through the sky were three beautiful swans. Silver and Cara stepped back as the swans landed in the Spectacular Library of Magical Things. As they landed they shapeshifted into women with long red hair. The women had long slender necks and wings stretched out from their shoulder blades.

One of the women stepped toward Cara and Silver. "My name is Ríona. I am Queen of the Soul Dancers. These are my sisters Laoise and Fiadh. Our song has been trapped for years within this magical library. We are so grateful that you have set it free."

Silver bowed her head.

"The Soul Dancers are the rightful custodians of Banshee Island. It is an honour for me to welcome you here, Ríona. And there is someone here that I would like you all to meet. Cara is a Soul Dancer too."

Ríona gasped. She recognised the girl straight away. Her baby girl was called Cara. The child that was born with one wing. Ríona made a pact with a wicked witch called Spellfinder that if she was able to change into a human woman she could stay in the Land of the Living until her first daughter was born. However, then she must return to the Island of the Soul Dancers. It broke Ríona's heart to say goodbye to her husband

and newborn daughter. Séamus never knew the truth of why Ríona left. She could not believe how much Cara resembled him. She had inherited his black hair and large brown eyes. Ríona missed Séamus with all her heart.

"Cara, is that really you?"

"Mother?"

Cara bent her head and her mother wrapped both her wings around her. It felt comforting to be nestled beneath such large and powerful wings.

"I would like to welcome you all to Banshee Island," said Silver.

"We are delighted to be here."

Cara's right arm throbbed. It felt as though it had a heartbeat. She stepped back out of the embrace of her mother's wings.

"Cara, look! You are gaining your second wing!" said Silver.

Ríona, Laoise and Fiadh all stood around Cara. They surrounded her with their huge wings and sang their song. When they had finished singing they stepped backwards and revealed a magnificent sight. Cara had another wing. Her left arm had completely disappeared. Tears fell from her eyes like shooting stars.

"My beautiful daughter – you are a Soul Dancer just like us."

It was then that something caught Cara's eyes. "Silver, look." Cara pointed a wing towards the dark corner of the library. It was no longer there. The darkness was replaced with rows and rows of empty bookshelves. All waiting to be filled with magical things.

"Oh marvellous!" Silver cried aloud. "The Booley Girls must have found a way to escape from the Mists of Time, Cara! That means that Banshee Island will start to heal. The witches have no power over the island anymore. They will leave us in peace. The island's magic is too powerful for them. They won't survive here."

Cara was delighted. "That is wonderful news. Where will they go?"

"They will make their way back to the mainland and try to blend in with people in the Land of the Living. They will use their magic to get what they want."

"I bet Síofra had something to do with it. She was determined that she was going to rescue the Booley Girls and now that she has found her cry she is more powerful than ever."

A worried look crossed Silver's face like a storm cloud on a spring morning.

"I did not realise that Síofra had found her cry."

"Yes, it was on the night that I got injured in battle."

"That makes perfect sense. I hope she makes it home soon, Cara."

"Something tells me that she will find her way back to us."

Cara smiled at Silver. She felt stronger than ever before. More balanced now that she had gained her second wing. She opened her wings wide. Feathers flew through the air.

Ríona stretched her neck. Then she touched Cara's neck with the tips of her feathers. "There is so much I have to teach you, Cara. So much that you have to learn about Soul Dancing. Our journey together has only just begun."

Chapter thirty-four

THE GHOST GIRL RETURNS

Róisín stood beneath the oak tree that grew at the entrance to Daphney Castle. Two swans swam in the water beneath the bridge. She was relieved to have finally found her way home. It seemed as though she had been gone for a lifetime, although she knew that it could have only been a few days. It was so strange. One moment she was walking in dense fog, then suddenly the fog lifted and the moon shone down like a torch illuminating her way home. Róisín guessed that it was late. She hoped her mother was still awake – she always liked it when her mother read her a story at bedtime. She could not wait to see her twin brother Séamus. They had their thirteenth birthday celebrations to plan. It would be a great occasion. They were going to hold their party in Soul Shadow Manor. Róisín only wished for one thing for her birthday. She longed for Banshee Island to appear through the mist.

She knocked on the castle door three times.

"*Hold your horses!*" a voice that Róisín didn't recognise shouted – a woman's voice.

How peculiar, she thought. It is normally the job of the butler to answer the door.

The door slowly creaked open and a young woman stood there in a black dress with a white apron. Her eyes opened wide in disbelief, then she blessed herself.

The woman looked as though she had been crying.

"Good lord! You gave me a shock. You look just like Miss Cara," she said, then she blew her nose into a handkerchief. "Who are you?"

A breeze whistled in the trees and Róisín trembled. An owl was perched on a wall close by. It hooted to announce its presence.

"I am sorry to have scared you. I don't know anybody called Cara. This is my home."

"Your home? No, you must be mistaken. This castle belongs to Séamus O'Leary."

Róisín smiled. What was her twin brother thinking – telling the servants that he owned the castle?

"Séamus O'Leary is my twin brother. I am his sister Róisín."

Kitty was unable to speak. She stared at the young girl in disbelief. How could this be Róisín O'Leary? She was one of the Booley Girls. She disappeared without a trace thirty years ago.

"Good grief, Kitty! Don't stand there with the door open. You are letting in a terrible draft."

Róisín didn't recognise the man's voice. It didn't belong to her papa.

She pushed passed the woman at the door into the entrance hall and confronted the man inside.

"I don't know who you are but my name is Róisín O'Leary and I live here," she said.

Séamus O'Leary fell to his knees. His face was as white as a ghost. Tears fell from his eyes.

"Darling Róisín, is that really you?"

"Yes, it is, but who are ..." Then Róisín looked into the man's eyes. She would recognise them anywhere. Then there was the birthmark above his left eyebrow. There was no mistaking it. This man was her brother Séamus. But how could that be?

Kitty shut the door and walked calmly over to Róisín.

Séamus O'Leary stood up. "Kitty, I will go upstairs

and tell Mother. Wait a little while and then bring Róisín up to her bedroom."

Then he raced out of the room and up the stone steps that led to his mother's bedroom.

"Hello, Róisín. My name is Kitty. I work here now. You are one of the Booley Girls, aren't you?"

"Yes, I am. I mean I was but I got separated from the group. The mist was very heavy and I couldn't find my way back home. It felt as though I was lost forever."

"There is no easy way to say this, Róisín, but you have been missing for thirty years. You see how your brother has aged – and your mother is an old woman now – you must be prepared for that."

"Oh, Kitty! I have butterflies in my stomach."

"That is only natural, lass," Kitty said reassuringly. She could not believe how much Róisín resembled Cara. It was quite remarkable. The only difference was that Róisín didn't have a wing.

* * *

Upstairs Séamus had told his mother what had happened. Then he helped her out of bed. Her silver hair hung about her shoulders. Trembling, she clung to her son's arm.

"Oh, Séamus! Thirty years ago your sister went missing and you say she has finally found her way home."

"Yes, Mother. It is hard to take in. We lost Cara and now Róisín mysteriously arrives home. But, come, sit here by the fire. Kitty is bringing Róisín up."

He sat her down in an armchair and put her shawl about her shoulders.

Mrs O'Leary looked anxiously up at her son. Wrinkles stretched from the corners of her eyes.

"There is one thing that concerns me though."

"What is it, Mother?"

"It is stupid really."

"Please, Mother, tell me what is troubling you."

"It is just that I was a young and beautiful woman when your sister left. She might not recognise me now that I am old and grey."

"Nonsense! You are our mother. You will always be beautiful to us. It is worse for me. I have a twin sister who is thirty years younger than me!" Séamus laughed then he patted his mother on the arm.

A knock sounded at the door.

"There they are!"

He went and ushered Kitty and his sister in.

"Róisín! Is it really you?"

"Oh, Mother!" Róisín cried.

Then she ran and, kneeling by her mother's chair, she threw herself into her mother's open arms. "I missed you so much! Although I feel as though I only left here a few days ago."

"A lot has happened since you left, my darling girl. We have much to catch up on. But you are here now and that is all that matters."

"Where is Father? I so want to see him!"

Tears gathered like raindrops in Mrs O'Leary's eyes.

"Oh, my beautiful girl, your father passed away many years ago. I am so sorry."

"No, say it isn't true! I never got to say goodbye to him."

Róisín placed her head against her mother's shoulder. It felt so good to be home but hard to believe that she would never see her father again.

Séamus hated to see his sister so sad. He placed his hand on her head.

"The last thing I remember is that we were planning a huge celebration for our thirteenth birthday, Róisín. Would you like to pick up where we left off?"

"Oh Séamus! I would love that!" Róisín cried and, jumping to her feet, she hugged him.

"Great! We will have a grand celebration next week in Soul Shadow Manor. All of the Booley Girls are invited, of course."

"Dear brother, it feels so good to be back home!"

"Kitty, would you show Róisín to her old bedroom, please? Everything is exactly as she left it but you'll need to light a fire there and put fresh bedclothes on the bed. And help her find something suitable to wear –"

"Don't worry, sir," Kitty cut in. "I'll take care of her."

"And, Róisín, come back here then and we'll find you something to eat. I'm sure you're hungry."

"I am, brother!" Róisín said with a laugh.

Séamus and Rose O'Leary watched Róisín walk away. They both breathed a huge sigh of relief. Their ghost girl was home at last.

Chapter thirty-five

TOGETHER AGAIN

Síofra's mind raced. So much had happened she could scarcely take it in. Her eyes shifted to her mother who was steering the wheel of the small red fishing boat. Guiding them both home. Her long white hair fell across her shoulders. Foamy waves crashed over the small red boat like foamy, white fingers. If only Cara could see me now, Síofra thought. It had crossed her mind that Cara's soul might arrive on Banshee Island. However, Cara was no ordinary girl. She was unique. A Soul Dancer. Soul Dancers had not been on Banshee Island since the witches stole their song. Síofra would give anything just to see her friend one last time.

She smiled at her mother. She could not wait for Silver to see her sister again.

"We should be there soon, Síofra."

"Yes, Mother." Síofra took her silver spyglass from her satchel and peered through it. Her heart leapt. Her fingers twitched. She screamed with excitement.

"Síofra, be careful, you will fall overboard!"

However, Síofra could not contain her delight. Tears of joy fell from her eyes. There on the shore stood Silver. She was holding Niamh in her arms. The animal's red coat glistened in the sunlight.

Then beside them stood an extraordinary girl. Her pale-blue dress billowed in the breeze. Her silky black hair danced over her shoulders. Her large eyes were tucked beneath dark eyelashes like secrets. Waves lapped against her ankles. It was Cara the Soul Dancer. Síofra gasped when she realised that Cara had two wings instead of one. Long white feathers stretched like clouds from her shoulder blades. They were as smooth as the translucent sea glass that washed up on the shore.

"Cara, you came home!" Síofra cried. She could not wait any longer. She took off her pirate hat and unlaced her boots. Then she jumped overboard. She wrestled with the waves and swam as fast as she could towards the shore. Beneath the magical sea were birds that could swim. In the sky above her head were fish that could fly. Banshee Island was thriving again.

"Síofra, I am here!" Cara shouted as she ran out into the waves.

"Careful, Cara. Your feathers will get wet!" Silver shouted.

But Cara didn't care. All she wanted was to see Síofra again. They had made a promise that they would always be there for each other and it was a promise that they both intended to keep. They ran towards each other, laughing and splashing in the waves. Síofra and Cara were together and nothing would ever come between then again. The spectacular journey of the Banshee and the Soul Dancer had only just begun.

ENDS

Also by Poolbeg.com

Now that you're hooked,
why not try

The Legend of
Valentine
Sorrow

Caroline Busher

Here's a sneak preview
of Chapter 1

Chapter One

County Sligo, August 1832

VAMPIRES APPEAR

"Do you hear him, Father?"

Clarabell flew closer to her father and pointed at the town far below where many bonfires burned.

"I want him, Father. Can we take him home with us?"

The sound of the boy crying came from a house blanketed in fog on the street below.

Luca would do anything for his daughter, and he realized that he had spoiled her for the past two hundred years. Clarabell had every luxury that a twelve-year-old girl could dream of. Brightly coloured dresses that were cut from the finest silk and adorned with ostrich feathers. Coats and hats made of velvet.

Mechanical birds-of-paradise, that sang to her from golden cages. Dolls of every description, with outfits to match her own. The only thing she didn't have was a brother or sister. Loneliness was taking its toll on her.

"No, Clarabell. We must leave the boy where he is. Death will take him – it is the natural way."

It was too late. Clarabell swooped through the clouds. Within seconds she was standing on the tower of Sligo Abbey, arms outstretched. Her red-velvet cloak, adorned with emeralds, was blowing in the breeze. Her blue eyes pierced the darkness. Sligo town stretched before her like a dream. Mist rose from the Garavogue river. Smoke rose from chimney stacks and bonfires, and lamps lit the streets.

Clarabell launched into the air and landed with a thud outside the abbey where tombstones covered in moss protruded from the earth like crooked teeth.

"*I am coming for you!*" Clarabell cried. Then she ran along the cobbled streets until she came to a house on Old Market Street. Placing her gloved hand on the door, she pushed it open. The house was cold, and the walls were damp.

Clarabell stood as still as a statue and watched from the shadows as a boy of about her own age knelt by the bed of his lifeless mother. He held her hand, gripped her fingers and stared into her eyes, willing her to be alive.

He was perfect. His head of black curls matched her blonde curls, and his tear-filled eyes were the colour of the ocean on a summer's day.

Valentine sensed her presence beside him and flinched.

Cholera had spread through Sligo town like a secret. People tried to keep the disease away by burning fires and saying prayers, but nothing worked. Then the vampires came. Valentine had sensed them moving silently through the town. They were in the shadows that danced across the walls, in the silent breeze that blew the cloth on the window. They waited in the darkness until his mother took her last breath and now, he knew, they had come for him.

Then he saw her. Not a vampire, just a pale young girl. She could not have been more than twelve years old.

"Are you my Guardian Angel?" he gasped.

Clarabell giggled behind her cupped hand. Her blue eyes danced with delight. She had never been referred to as an angel before.

"I have come to save you."

"No, Clarabell. I forbid you."

A man appeared in the doorway. His skin was deathly pale.

Valentine screamed as the man approached the girl and gripped her by the wrist, anger flashing in his eyes.

She opened her mouth to scream and revealed sharp white teeth.

Valentine let go of his mother's cold hand. She had been in the County Fever Hospital until recent days. However, there weren't enough beds to cater for all the patients suffering from cholera and she had been sent home to die. His seventeen-year-old sister Matilda had remained in the hospital. He had said goodbye to her the previous evening as the sun set in the sky, knowing that they might never meet again.

"I will miss you, Valentine."

"You'll be home soon, Tilly. I think you're recovering – you're better than you were."

"I don't know about that, Valentine." Matilda reached into her pocket and handed him a small red cloth heart. The word *Hope* was embroidered on it with silver thread. She pressed it into the palm of his hand.

A tear slid down his pale cheek.

"Keep my heart safe until we meet again, dear brother."

Matilda's hair was golden, and people always

remarked on how kind she was. Valentine felt proud of his sister. She was good at sums and her favourite thing to do was to help her mother with the cooking and cleaning. Valentine had already lost his father and his younger brother Joe to cholera but saying goodbye to Matilda broke his heart.

"Come to me, boy!" Clarabell cried.

He blinked away thoughts of Matilda.

Full of sorrow, he walked over to the girl. He was powerless to resist. His heart was pounding loud and fast.

Luca, the Vampire King, was outraged. Then a sound outside the house and the unmistakable scent of wild roses alerted him to danger.

"Vampire Hunters! They have followed us here!" he hissed.

Clarabell had led them into danger. He had known that the cholera epidemic in County Sligo would attract every vampire in the kingdom. This meant that Vampire Hunters would soon follow. He had been foolish to allow Clarabell to accompany him tonight. He knew that they must go right away. If that meant taking the boy with them, then so be it. Now was not the time for one of Clarabell's temper tantrums. It would lead the Vampire Hunters straight to them.

"Bring the boy if you must, Clarabell. But hurry, it is not safe here."

"Wait! I can't go yet!" said Valentine.

He stepped back from Clarabell and looked around his house one last time. It was the only home he had ever known. He would miss the wooden kitchen table where he ate his dinner every night. He looked at his father's spectacles on the mantelpiece and his sister's embroidery on the rocking chair. Then he knelt beside his mother and kissed her gently on the forehead.

"Goodbye, Mother," he whispered into her ear. Then he said a little prayer. It was unbearable to think that he would never see her beautiful smile again. A tear trickled down his cheek.

Valentine did not know who these strange-looking people were or where they were taking him, but at that moment it seemed a safer option than waiting for cholera to claim his life.

He unclasped the heart-shaped locket from his mother's neck. It contained miniature paintings of his parents. He placed it in his pocket. Wherever he went, it would always remind him of them.

"We must leave right away." Luca stood in the doorframe with arms outstretched like a giant bat.

Clarabell ran like lightning to Valentine's side. She

snipped off a lock of his hair with her sharp fingernail and put it into a hidden pocket in her cloak. Then she gripped his wrist tightly and pulled it towards her lips. "I'm sorry for what I am about to do, but you will be mine forever," she said and sank her teeth into his wrist, until she could taste his blood.

Valentine pulled his arm free. A purple bruise bloomed like a flower around the toothmarks in his wrist. He felt faint. *"Get away from me!"* he cried.

Clarabell caught him in her arms and Valentine could feel the energy drain from his body. The entire room spun and he threw his arms around Clarabell's neck.

"I will protect you!" she cried as her feet rose off the ground.

Luca stood to one side to allow his daughter and her victim to escape through the open door.

Valentine tightened his grip on Clarabell's neck. Within seconds they were flying high. Afraid to utter another word, Valentine peered over Clarabell's shoulder. All the houses on his street came into view. Sligo was laid before him. The abbey, the gaol, and the River Garavogue which flowed through the ancient town. Then he saw the fever hospital, where his brother and father had died. He thought of Matilda and prayed that she was still alive. He saw his old schoolroom and the graveyard where generations of his family were laid to rest.

Angry men ran after them. They shot flaming arrows towards the sky in a desperate attempt to stop them.

Moments later, Clarabell and Valentine were flying over the Atlantic Ocean. The waves were as black as ink.

"I must be dreaming! This isn't real!" Valentine cried. Then he noticed his wrist and the purple bruise that had formed there, and he knew that he hadn't imagined it. What was happening to him was real and he might never see his mother, Matilda or his home in Sligo again.

The early-morning sun erupted on the horizon, and Valentine shivered. He had never felt so cold before. It felt as though pins and needles prickled his entire body. The gentle trickle of orange light stung his eyes.

Clarabell hissed. She felt it too.

Suddenly the sky was filled with hundreds of bats. They surrounded the children, shielding them from the light of the sun.

"Look, Valentine! They have come for us!"

Valentine blinked, and when he looked again the bats had turned into astonishing creatures with black capes.

305

They led them towards an island made of rock and shaped like a skull. It stood alone in the middle of the ocean. Waves slapped against the shore.

A sense of calm overcame Valentine as they descended upon the stones. It felt good to have his feet back on solid ground once more, though he didn't know where the creatures had taken him.

Clarabell bit down hard on her bottom lip. She knew that she had overstepped the line this time and that she might be punished for it by her father. She hoped that the other vampires wouldn't hurt the boy.

Her father Luca, the Vampire King, appeared before her. Lightning pierced the air. Thunder rolled from the sky. Then Luca led them down some stone steps, into a dark cave. A vampires' lair.